# HERALDIC DESIGN

# HERALDIC

## A HANDBOOK FOR

BY

WITH A FOREWORD BY

## A. COLIN COLE ESQ

PORTCULLIS PURSUIVANT OF ARMS

GENEALOGICAL PUBLISHING CO., INC.
BALTIMORE, 1976

# DESIGN

## STUDENTS

### HEATHER CHILD

*First published 1965*
*Reprinted, with corrections, 1966*
*Reprinted offset, 1970*


Reprinted by
Genealogical Publishing Co., Inc.
Baltimore, 1976
In cooperation with
G. Bell and Sons, Ltd.


Library of Congress Catalogue Card Number 66-31918
International Standard Book Number 0-8063-0071-X

*Made in the United States of America*

# FOREWORD

## by A. Colin Cole, Esq., Portcullis Pursuivant of Arms

There is today and there has been for some time an awakening of interest in heraldry both as an art and a science, accompanied by greater understanding of its practical and decorative purposes when at its feudal height in war and peace than was the case when last there was an upsurge of interest on a comparable scale, at the time of the Gothic revival a dozen decades ago. The patina of romantic fantasy that then it bore and the misleading legends upon which it was nourished by its publicists induced such distortion that the realities of the ancient art and science were scarcely discernible amid the euphoria and virtually all effort at artistic expression was productive only of what was as grotesque as it was ugly, as debased as it was dull and depressing.

Yet interest in heraldry survived and, aided by the researches of historically minded writers, has broken through to fresh pinnacles of knowledge, albeit as yet unmatched by similar achievement in pictorial and other forms of practical display.

It is in the hope of being able to redress this unbalance that Miss Child's book has been written, and also as a result of a conviction, resulting from many hours of conversation between the author and the writer of this foreword, during which they were increasingly conscious of an exciting unanimity of ideas in this respect, that in the field of heraldic art and design there remained some blighted patches that needed tending before it could be said that everything in the heraldic garden was lovely.

Thus, while heraldry should be viewed in its twofold aspect of science and art, the emphasis of this book is on the latter, although the message of the text is also that artistic excellence cannot be achieved without a grasp of heraldry's other characteristic coupled with awareness of its origins, its pristine forms, and the discipline imposed by the fact that in Great Britain it is administered by official authority stemming from the Crown.

Heraldry is old, and its growth as a combined art and science derives from its antiquity and (when it was better known as armory) from its nature in that it was expressed by devices depicted upon banners and shields of arms that in life were carried by their owners, and a little later, by devices that were worn upon helms guarding the heads of the men who carried those same shields and banners. To model such a man as did the sculptor in effigy upon a tomb, was to shape him in life-like proportions with his shield as he had carried it and as it had been made, having length and breadth, resting his head upon or near his helm with the crest thereon, this carved in stone as something that, nine times out of ten, in life had had added to it when formed, to the two dimensions it shared with the shield, a third, that of depth of body.

To depict such a man's armorials, his shield, helm and crest with the further attributes of torse or crest crown, mantling and sometimes supporters to uphold the shield, all these comprising his Achievement, is for the artist illuminating a vellum scroll, designing an heraldic bookplate or seal matrix, or painting a panel, quite another task, for it is one being attemp.ed primarily in the flat, not in the round, and his problem is different from that of the sculptor or wood-carver; for confined within the space of length and breadth of his medium, a piece of vellum, a sheet of paper, the surface of a piece of wood, he has to reproduce not only the one prime element of the Achievement that has two dimensions, the shield, but to marry this in one plane with the other, disparate elements, the three-dimensional helm and crest with their accompanying torse or crest crown, mantling and perhaps supporters.

It is no exaggeration (for this is a factor that is and has been neglected) to assert that the extent to which the artist succeeds in this difficult task of composing what may be called the three unities, of helm, crest and shield, is one of the most important of the measures by which his work can be judged as meritorious or negligible; Miss Child's book will go far to help him to succeed in this and also in regard to many other points by which his heraldic artistry falls to be tested.

There are indeed many such points, but I have chosen to concentrate upon that which concerns the relationship between helm, crest and shield, because this seems to me to be fundamental if heraldry in art as well as official heraldry as an art is to be accorded the acclaim that both are capable of, as a beautiful, practical and still meaningful expression of an ancient art that is also a continuing discipline.

In this book another fundamental is the regard which artists are urged to have for the inspiring heraldic display of the early days of armory. The justification for this is best expressed in the words of W. St. John Hope, fifty years ago: 'Should it be thought that undue stress has been laid upon the pre-Tudor heraldry, to the comparative exclusion of that of later times, it may be pointed out that until the principles of the earlier heraldry have been grasped and appreciated, it is impossible to get rid of the cast-iron uniformity and stupid rules that bound the heraldry of today and tend to strangle all attempts to raise it to a higher level.'

This is strongly put, and fortunately the position has improved since St. John Hope's day, there being now relatively less ignorance by artists of examples of heraldic design of surpassing excellence that have survived from the medieval period, but it might be argued that heraldic art, in its most frequent manifestation, that is to say, on paper or flat material of some kind, has become by now so divorced from the actuality of its sources, it is so much *sui generis*, that in the sphere of 'paper heraldry' the problem of the dimensional clash that has been posed has no relevance and further that the proper relationship between say, helm and crest can be ignored so that crests that would never have been worn in fact, for example crest beasts that leap sideways off an affronty helm are acceptable. Such assertions I can meet only with a direct demurrer and reference to this book in the hope that it will prove more persuasive than I.

Those that turn to this book will not need to be convinced that 'there is something in all this heraldry that from the beginning has touched us with a charm not easily to be explained, something in the simple souls of men is pleasured by those bright reds and blues and golds, those beasts and birds, and bars and bends and crosses, seen bright in the glass of a chapel window or faded on an ancient skin of parchment', but to those pleasures they will be able to add that of trying for themselves to match the best work of past and present and with skill based on technical knowledge, a dash of imagination, a sense of history and some practice, possibly even will outstrip those hitherto acknowledged as masters of heraldic design and of the art of herald painting.

# ACKNOWLEDGEMENTS

I am grateful to all those who have lent material for the illustrations and to the many writers and heraldic artists whose works I have consulted.

I wish to express my appreciation to A. Colin Cole, Esq., Portcullis Pursuivant of Arms, for reading the manuscript and for his many helpful suggestions.

I should like to thank Dorothy Colles and Ann Hechle for their patience and practical assistance.

H. C.

*Note on the Second Edition:* The author would like to thank her many correspondents who have suggested improvements in text and illustrations. As many of these amendments as practicable have been included in the second edition, 1966.

# CONTENTS

# A NOTE ON THE ILLUSTRATIONS

The half-tone plates illustrate examples from the main sources of early heraldry: seals, rolls of arms, heraldic memorials, armorial carvings, stained glass and embroidery. They also illustrate heraldry in use today and include many styles of heraldic design in different crafts and for a wide variety of purposes.

The line drawings are closely related to points in the text, they include historical examples and coats of arms in current use, they have been drawn in outline for clarity of detail.

A representative example of civic heraldry has been chosen for discussion, that of the Westminster City Council, both for its historical associations and for the variety and interest of the charges. The heraldic features are analysed in progressive order beginning with the shield; as each item is discussed the setting out of the drawing is explained and variations given. Thus every part of a full achievement, shield, helmet, crest, mantling and supporters is analysed and some of the basic problems of design are considered. This plan keeps the finished design and the details related to one another and to other illustrations in the book; further developments follow naturally from the initial survey of the problem.

# THE PLATES

# THE DRAWINGS

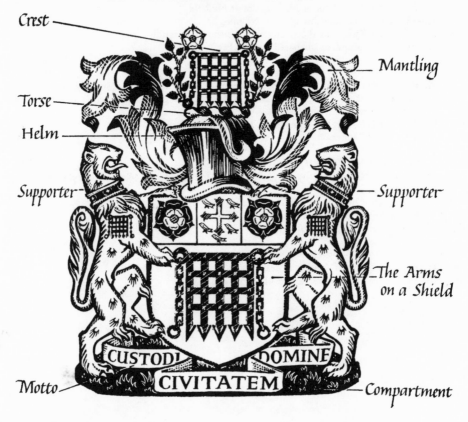

Crest

Mantling

Torse

Helm

Supporter

Supporter

The Arms
on a Shield

CUSTODI DOMINE
CIVITATEM

Motto

Compartment

## The armorial bearings of Westminster City Council

Arms of Westminster City Council drawn on scraper board

**BLAZON**

ARMS: Azure, a portcullis or, on a chief of the second a pale of the first thereon a cross flory between five martlets also of the second, being the Arms of King Edward the Confessor, between two united roses gules and argent

CREST: On a wreath of the colours or and azure a portcullis chained sable between on the dexter side a rose gules and on the sinister a rose argent both barbed, seeded, stalked, leaved and erect proper

SUPPORTERS: On either side a lion ermine, that on the dexter gorged with a collar or, thereon three roses gules barbed and seeded also proper, that on the sinister with a collar azure, thereon as many roses argent also barbed and seeded proper and each charged on the body with a portcullis chained or

*The old City of Westminster ceased to exist on 31st March 1965. The arms granted to the City of Westminster incorporate features from the Arms of the three superseded authorities*

# INTRODUCTION

The aim of this book is to give the student of design sufficient information about the structure and detail of heraldic insignia to enable him to produce well balanced designs of coats of arms.    In pursuit of this aim it is necessary to become familiar with the more common heraldic terms and to know where to refer for further information.    The science and grammar of heraldry have been clearly set out in other works and some of those most helpful to designers are included in the short list of books on page 175.

The design of heraldry and its decorative aspect have not been so fully covered by writers on heraldic subjects.    Many who need to draw arms for their own use or for commissioned work do not know where to look for helpful basic information. In this book the author has tried to give a sufficient account of the heraldic terms to make it a practical handbook on its own.    Blazons have been given of examples illustrated in the text and the reader is directed to some of the varied sources of applied heraldry.    The notes on working out an achievement are the fruit of experience acquired in painting arms and the study of heraldic art and reading on the subject.

Why, it may be asked, should anyone need to design a coat of arms in the second half of the 20th century?    The answer has its roots in the development of early heraldry more than nine hundred years ago, and the enduring prestige of tradition in our social structure, of which prestige heraldry is itself a symbol.

It is the writer's belief that the apparently anachronistic interest in heraldry—more widespread today than ever before—is in large part due to the deep and instant appeal of visual symbols.    In an age when people are surfeited with too much printed matter it is a relief to turn to a vivid picture language such as heraldry, with its framework of rules, variety of detail and romantic historical associations.

The original intention of heraldic devices was firstly to establish ownership, as in the use of seals (Figs. 1 and 2); and secondly to establish identity, as on the field of war or in tournaments (Fig. 3).    When arms became hereditary the bearing of them signified continuity and a worthy pedigree.    So the coat of arms has come to be a

Fig. 1. Seal of Sir Thomas de Beauchamp, 3rd Earl of Warwick.   Date of seal 1344

Fig. 4. A Knight and his chained Lady representing the matrimonial ties between husband and wife and also their heraldic links.   From a painting in a 15th-century manuscript

Fig. 2. Seal of Sir Richard de Beauchamp, 5th Earl of Warwick.   Date of seal 1401

Fig. 3. *Left:* Knights jousting, from a coloured MS. compiled by Sir Thomas Wriothesley, Garter King of Arms, 1504 to 1534
*Right:* Knights jousting, from a 16th-century MS.

mark of historical identity and family continuity, transcending the individual bearer (Fig. 4). Is it then so surprising to find that the modern usages of heraldry have their most popular developments in public activities?

The coats of arms of corporate bodies such as county councils, boroughs, banks and limited liability companies are probably better known than those of any single individual except the arms of the Sovereign, and Royal Arms are a symbol of Monarchy itself.

The designer will find that modern enterprises, such as the B.B.C. and the Atomic Energy Authority, both without the least historical or military connections, desire and obtain the stability of tradition and the mark of identity conferred by the possession of heraldic insignia (Plate 21 and Fig. 5).

UNITED KINGDOM ATOMIC ENERGY

AUTHORITY

Fig. 5. Armorial Bearings of the United Kingdom Atomic Energy Authority: Sable, semy of Plates (representing the atomic pile, a block of graphite into which uranium rods have been inserted), a Pile barry dancetty or and gules (symbolizing nuclear fission taking place within the atomic pile).
Crest: on a wreath argent and sable a Sun in splendour of 32 points or, charged with a voided Escutcheon gules therein a Martlet sable. (The sun symbol of heat and energy is charged with emblems from the arms of Lord Rutherford).
Supporters: On either side a Pantheon gules unguled or, semy of Mullets 13 of 6 points 2 of 7 and gorged with a Crown palisado affixed thereto and reflexed over the back a chain gold. (The Pantheon is a rare heraldic beast spangled with stars and symbolizing the natural forces of the universe, the points of the stars on each Pantheon total 92, the number of electrons in uranium. The crown palisado deriving from the palisade of a fortified enclosure, in conjunction with the chain attached, symbolizes control and the harnessing of the atom to many purposes.)

It is a touching thought that as the new countries of Africa and Asia ripen into political independence, their national pride demands not only a national anthem, but elaborate coats of arms, bearing, it is true, emblems that can be widely understood by their simpler peoples, but blazoned according to the ancient heraldic rules of a European tradition nearly a thousand years old (Fig. 6).

*The Arms of* KENYA

Fig. 6. The arms of KENYA: Per fess sable and vert on a fess gules fimbriated argent a cock grasping in the dexter claw an axe also argent and for supporters on either side a lion or grasping in the interior fore paw a spear of estate, the hafts of the spears crossed in saltire behind the shield, the whole upon a compartment representing Mount Kenya proper together with the motto HARAMBEE

We are perhaps more aware of the emotional power of symbolism from which modern heraldry derives its life than our immediate forebears were. It is what heraldry stands for, rather than the devices of which it is composed, that gives public bodies the desire to own armorial bearings. The undeniable appeal of symbolism is extended when it is supported by a commonly understood religious or military system. Christians everywhere, for example, understand the symbolism of the Cross but where there is no generally accepted vocabulary of symbols the work of a designer—who desires to associate his decorative motifs with emotional meaning—is impoverished.

Although it would be folly to claim that the practice, rules and grammar of heraldry are now widely understood, they are certainly accepted, so that the citizen sees nothing comic in the brightly coloured coat of arms of his local authority on the municipal dust-cart.

It is the general acceptance of heraldry, in this country at any rate, that brings us back to our attempt to answer the questions: 'Why should a contemporary designer need to know how to design a coat of arms today?   In what fields of activity is the designer called on to use heraldic decoration?'

*The Activity of the Designer Today*

There could be said to be two principal modes of heraldic design, namely flat design, for use on paper, glass, china, banners, panels, transfers, and the like, contrasting with sculptural design in relief, carried out in wood, stone, metal or plastic and generally used on buildings for architectural decoration.   These two types of design may be divided again into two further fields; firstly, commissions for private individuals and, secondly, commissions for public bodies or holders of office in their public capacities such as mayors, heads of colleges and directors of companies.   The second of these two fields is much the larger and usually offers the designer more range and reward.

The most general uses of heraldic design are perhaps on our commonest means of exchange: coinage and sometimes on stamps, also for activities of bodies associated with the Crown, such as the Royal Mint, H.M. Stationery Office (Fig. 107), and the Office of Works and Public Buildings, all of which include the use of the Royal Arms.   Traders who enjoy royal patronage, and who are recognized as providing goods for the use of members of the Royal Family, are entitled to display the Royal Arms, being Royal Warrant holders.   The temporary pageantry of coronations, royal weddings and state visits also incorporates the gay display of arms, crests and badges.

Private people today prefer not to show off the possession of armorial bearings. With the exception of small objects such as bookplates, cuff links, signet rings, engraved silver, pedigrees on vellum or small framed library paintings, there is not a great deal made of opportunities for the display of private arms.

In public and corporate activities, however, there are numerous opportunities for enterprising craftsmen to make designs for use both on flat surfaces and in relief. In civic buildings such as libraries, halls, colleges, schools and hospitals the use of heraldry for decoration is likely both for its gaiety, its social value in engendering pride and also, and more practically, because it is less controversial and of more permanent significance than other daring and original art forms or decorative schemes, often ephemeral, which despite a frequent deliberate striving for the contemporary, sometimes find it harder to win the necessary approval of the committees concerned.

The designing of stained glass windows for commemorative purposes is a fine occasion for the use of heraldry and there are excellent modern examples of these in churches, colleges and halls.

There are recurring opportunities for the display of heraldry in the presentation of gifts or honours from corporate bodies to individuals; and from individuals to bodies with which they are long associated; also from loyal bodies and individuals to the Sovereign on ceremonial occasions, and from the Sovereign to visiting Heads of State.

In the great majority of cases apt and newly minted symbols are hard for the designer to invent and the existing symbolism of heraldry can be adapted with wit, ingenuity and life to the enrichment of the gift whatever its material may take. These gifts may be in silver with heraldic insignia sumptuously enamelled, engraved or chased, and some fine examples are included in the illustrations of contemporary work. The beauty of engraving on glass is increasingly valued for formal gifts. The illumination with gold leaf and rich pigments of manuscripts on vellum or parchment has a long history, and heraldic devices make splendid decorations for illuminated addresses, freedom scrolls and similar unique works.

Designs may be required to be worked in embroidery for use in cathedrals and churches or in public places where the display of rich materials is appropriate.

*The Requirements of the Designer*

We now turn from the scope for heraldic design to the requirements of a designer and his problems, and for these some understanding of the rules of heraldry is a prerequisite.

The main principles of the grammar of heraldry can be mastered in a short time with the aid of a reliable handbook. The colours and metals employed are few and the forms used should be simple and clearly identified.

Heraldic drawing looks deceptively easy but it is in fact very difficult to do well. The nice choice of shapes for shields, the placing of charges on them, the proportion and balance of the various parts and the lines which give strength and unity to the whole come with experience and the study of sound examples.

A good heraldic design is invalidated if it is not an accurate interpretation of the blazon. It is hard for the beginner to know how much freedom the artist is permitted in making his drawing or by what rules he is bound. If the space available does not allow the whole achievement to be included it is not easy to discover which of the different elements constituting a coat of arms must be shown, and how they may be rearranged. 'The statement which heraldry makes is a very definite one, its accuracy should be the first care, this vital consideration is frequently lost sight of'. It is well worth while to take trouble to design heraldry both accurately and well. Some admirable artists fail to appreciate this need. Even within this comparatively rigid framework there is room for a personal approach and the answers to some of these problems are put forward in this book.

Originality is not the outstanding characteristic quality of heraldic design, which is a derivative art. Dignity and vitality are qualities the designer would do well to cultivate. Sir George Bellew has said 'Heraldry is vulnerable to ridicule' and the designer should avoid a flippant interpretation of blazon unless he is seeking to display the lighter side of the art as in the delightful illustrations to 'Simple Heraldry Cheerfully Illustrated' by Iain Moncreiffe and Don Pottinger. The enjoyment of the designer in his work will depend on his understanding what it is that he is designing, otherwise he will be compelled merely to copy a previous design of the blazon.

The use of insignia that was formerly worn, to mark today's corporate owner-ship may seem anomalous, but it is well to remember that a coat of arms was once a series of solid objects. These were: a shield with charges on it; a helmet with a crest in wood or leather; the mantling and a crest wreath. Although much heraldic design is mainly graphic it is wise and vital to good design to keep clearly in mind the substance and nature of the actual objects; only thus will be avoided some of the sillier corruptions of bewildered draughtsmen.

The necessary background of knowledge to enable the artist to design a coherent coat of arms is more easily learnt if enthusiasm reinforces bookwork. The study of heraldry is also the study of the history of the crafts which display it. The source material is more fully dealt with in the section on 'Sources of Heraldic Design'. Briefly, however, it lies in the surviving monuments and treasures of cathedrals, abbeys, churches and colleges and in seals, enamels, stained glass, embroidery, manuscripts, precious metals and even in arms and armour.

It is widely held that the noblest heraldic designs are those of the anonymous craftsmen of the Middle Ages whose works in metal and stone show a breadth and simplicity later to be lost and a mastery of balance and space-filling hard to emulate. In these early days of heraldry, when shields were used in battle or tournament and helmets were worn on the head and carried crests of modelled leather, all heraldry was 'possible', but with the decline of heraldry in the round fantastic crests were devised that could never have been supported on a helm.

The later more florid style in coats of arms in Tudor and Stuart times are of interest heraldically but less satisfying to the purist of design. After its brilliant medieval period the art of heraldry suffered a long decadence.

It is therefore important for a designer to be able to visualize his designs in three dimensions so that they could function in space, not only for designing in relief, but also for painting on a flat surface (Fig. 64). He should have at least an outline knowledge of styles of ornament and of armour and its periods of development.

Some understanding of anatomy is necessary so as to give strength and movement to the drawing of figures and heraldic beasts. A sense of stylization is valuable, as heraldic symbols are not the same as the naturalistic renderings of objects.

Some knowledge of the development of styles enables a designer to avoid those mistakes that spring from ignorance of history. A timid herald painter tends to copy the models of previous artists and such copyists rarely excel, but generally detract from the originals, and their products become stereotyped. Fortified by an understanding of the historical background and a knowledge of the rules the designer will find the confidence and inspiration to make vigorous designs of his own.

An artist should never forget that he is endeavouring to overcome a most challenging problem—to marry, in a design that is two-dimensional (having length and breadth) objects that themselves vary in their dimensions, that is a helm and crest being three-dimensional, and a shield of arms essentially of two dimensions. This is a problem that a carver understands and one that a designer in the flat must grasp if he is to produce satisfying and technically accurate work.

# PART ONE

## THE GRANTING OF ARMS

Heraldry, or more accurately armory, which became established as a system during the second half of the 12th century, was at first mainly utilitarian. The devices displayed on shields and later as crests, on surcoats, horse bardings and banners, served to distinguish armoured combatants in war and in tournament; when used on seals they were marks of identity. Arms were at first a sign of the greater nobility, but by the mid-13th century they were also extensively used by lesser nobility,

Fig. 7. Armed equestrian figure, similar in design to those on seals, from a fragment of 13th-century needlework in coloured silk on linen. A banderole, forerunner of the mantling, is attached to the fan-shaped crest. The field of the shield, crest, surcoat, banderole and trapper are all diapered

knights and those who later came to be styled gentlemen. By the mid-14th century the principle that no man might use arms already adopted by another had been assumed in an English court of law and it was not long before the Crown forbade the bearing of arms without authority. The position today is that in addition to grants of arms by Royal Warrant, arms and armorial insignia are granted only by the Kings of Arms in England, by Lyon King of Arms in Scotland and Ulster King of Arms in Northern Ireland. The Kings of Arms have the power to grant by letters patent, a power conferred on them individually by the Crown.

The College of Arms has thirteen members—three Kings of Arms: Garter, Clarenceux and Norroy; six Heralds: Lancaster, Chester, York, Richmond, Windsor and Somerset; and four Pursuivants: Bluemantle, Portcullis, Rouge Croix and Rouge Dragon; all are officers of the Royal Household and appointed by the Crown on the nomination of the Duke of Norfolk, Earl Marshal of England.

Apart from their duties on State occasions the members of the College investigate claims to bear arms, arrange for the granting of armorial bearings, draw up family trees and trace pedigrees. The practice of heraldry and genealogy has been closely linked since Tudor times.

The unrivalled heraldic collections in the record rooms and libraries of the College of Arms in Queen Victoria Street are not available for direct consultation by the public, their use requiring expert knowledge. Enquiries by members of the public, either in person or by letter, are dealt with by the officer of arms 'in waiting', that is to say on duty for the week. Officers receive only a nominal salary and fees are charged to clients for their services; an estimate of the cost of the work advised will be given. The College employs a number of herald painters and scriveners who engross patents of arms, pedigrees and records.

The sole right to arms is established by Letters Patent of Grants from the Kings of Arms, or by Warrant from the Crown, or by inheritance by lineal descent from an ancestor to whom a Grant was made, or whose right to arms has been officially recognized and registered in a way conversant with the laws of Arms as practised in this country. As regards eligibility, it has been said and broadly speaking holds good that 'any worthy man of good repute and adequate substance may apply for and most probably will receive a grant of arms for himself and his family'. While much the same applies to certain corporate bodies, those which are purely commercial are not normally eligible unless they are leaders in their respective fields and their operations are of national importance.

All 'Grants' or 'Confirmations of Arms' are formally and regularly recorded, with a full blazon of the insignia, at the College of Arms. When letters patent are issued to an individual person, or corporate body, the official description, or blazon, of the arms is engrossed on vellum, accompanied by a comparably attractive illumination of the arms in the margin of the patent (Plates 11, 15). The blazon is the important factor for the artist to consider first in any heraldic design he may be called upon to make; it is from this official description of the arms that he makes his own interpretation in his own style, bearing in mind from the start the purpose for which his design is intended and the materials in which it is to be carried out. These same arms may require to be displayed in many different ways: painted, engraved, carved, embroidered and so on, and the craftsman must use his skill to adapt the authorized version of the arms to such varied purposes.

The design for an heraldic inn sign (Plate 27) should obviously be simpler and bolder in its treatment than that used for an engraved book-plate. One should be recognizable from some distance away, the other is designed to be held in the hand. A fresh interpretation of the blazon should be made for each material. No more tedious mistake can be made than the forcing of amorial bearings, as depicted in a Patent of the Kings of Arms, to serve every purpose.

It is quite usual for people to expect, or even to insist, that the painting of their arms supplied officially by the College of Arms should be copied exactly as it stands, for fear that any alteration in the design will make it heraldically inaccurate. While it is helpful and often essential for a designer to see the official painting, as well as to read the blazon, he may have some difficulty in persuading his client that a fresh interpretation is desirable in order to make the design suit the purpose and the medium. The lazy designer tends to save himself trouble by merely transferring the official design into his medium.

# THE BLAZON

To paint or draw a coat of arms is to emblazon it, to describe a coat of arms in words is to blazon it.

When a contestant entered the lists at a tournament his presence was announced by the sound of a trumpet, after which the heralds declared his insignia, or in other words, blazoned his arms. The blazon therefore is the description of arms in technical language.

The language of early blazons was French or Latin. Later they became anglicized, except for a few technical terms. Gradually, blazons became extremely complicated with the addition of elaborate rules and at times they were almost unintelligible. As coats of arms lost their early simplicity and at the same time increased in number, it became important to describe each one precisely and accurately in words. Today there is an attempt to return to something of the earlier simplicity in both the composition and blazon of arms.

The intention of the written blazon is not to enable two persons to depict a coat of arms exactly similar in minute detail, but to enable each to render it correctly in all essentials, so that there is no doubt as to what is really intended. The wording of a Patent of Arms refers to the painting of the arms which accompanies it: '. . . as in the margin hereof more plainly depicted . . .', that is to say the painting is more legible than the technical wording of the blazon. It does not mean that the painting in the margin must be copied exactly in style by every artist depicting those arms. Of course one charge cannot be substituted for another, or its position fundamentally rearranged; nor can one metal or colour be changed for another, or the blazon would be compromised, but the style in which the insignia are drawn and coloured is at the discretion of the artist.

A designer should be familiar with the more common heraldic terms, so that on reading a blazon he can visualize a coat of arms he has never seen.

The reading of blazons should be practised until a technical description of a coat of arms can be written accurately and translated into a correct drawing. This skill is of importance to a designer, and excellent practice can be had by describing the arms in an illustrated 'Peerage' and subsequently checking the description from the blazon, or by making a drawing from the blazon and checking with the illustration.

Every blazon begins with the tincture of the field of the shield unless the field is divided, then the character of the division precedes the mention of the colour, e.g. 'Per pale or and gules'. Secondly, the principal charge or ordinary and its tincture are named. Then subsidiary charges and their tinctures and whether they are on or surrounding the principal charge or ordinary.

A 'trick' or quick sketch is a convenient way of noting essential heraldic facts (Fig. 8). An outline of the shield is made first and the heraldic details added in outline, together with a written abbreviation of their tinctures. The abbreviations used in blazon may not be short enough for a 'trick' and the following contractions can be substituted: O for Or; Ar for Argent; G for Gules; note B is used for Azure, since Az. and A may be easily confused with Ar.; S for Sable; Vt. for Vert. Charges which are duplicated may be indicated by numbers in a 'trick'.


# AN ACHIEVEMENT OF ARMS AND ITS COMPONENT PARTS

The terms 'arms', 'crest' and 'badge' tend to be used indiscriminately, although each has a distinct meaning, and it is necessary for the heraldic designer to know the names of the component parts of an achievement and to use them correctly.

A full display of armorial bearings is called an Achievement of Arms. Its component parts consist of:

1. THE ARMS: These are usually displayed upon a shield and are frequently called a coat of arms. In medieval times arms were displayed on the surcoat and upon horse trappings, as well as upon the shield. The term 'coat of arms' properly describes what would be displayed on a surcoat or tabard but by extension is applied to the insignia on a shield or banner, and it is often used as an alternative for the more accurate term 'Achievement of Arms'. The arms are the essential part of any achievement and they may constitute the whole armorial bearing. However, most personal and corporate arms carry a crest as well. The arms may be used alone without any other part of the achievement.

2. THE CREST: This is a device which should be depicted as carried upon a helm in association with the mantling and crest wreath. It is frequently and unhappily seen borne upon a crest wreath alone, both being divorced from the helm, a practice which has led more than any other to misunderstanding in designing new crests and depicting in a particular design those already existing. Crests are not used by women today.

3. THE SUPPORTERS: These are usually living creatures such as human beings, animals or birds, but may be monsters or imaginary creatures, which flank the shield and uphold it. They may be granted to Peers, Knights Grand Cross, and certain corporate bodies.

4. BADGES: These are supplementary devices sometimes repeating an element from the arms or crest, which can be displayed alone, or in association with the arms. They are not an integral part of the arms or crest.

5. THE MOTTO: It is usual to place the motto on a scroll or motto-tape beneath the shield. It is not usual for the motto to be included in the text of a Grant of Arms. In Scottish heraldry the motto is granted by letters patent and it flourishes above the shield about the crest; and where there are two mottoes, there are examples in English heraldry of those being shown on a scroll above and below the shield.

All heraldic figures and devices are termed charges whether they are placed on the shield or displayed in any other way. The shield, crest, mantling and supporters are said to be charged with any device placed upon them.

The coat of arms of the Westminster City Council is a handsome example ot civic heraldry which incorporates interesting historical associations, and clearly shows the component parts of an achievement.

The blazon given beneath the illustration on page 18 is the same wording as in the Patent of the Grant of Arms of 1902. At that time it was more usual than now in blazoning a tincture that recurs to refer to it indirectly, for example the blazon reads: '*Azure, a portcullis or, on a chief of the second* . . .' i.e. of the second tincture mentioned which is 'or', and again, '. . . *a cross flory between five martlets also of the second* . . .'. The portcullis, chief (Fig. 25), cross and martlets, therefore, are all gold, but the word 'or' is only mentioned once.    Similarly the term 'as many' takes the place of recurring numbers in a blazon.    It is essential for artists to interpret blazons correctly and this somewhat cumbersome wording is quite easy to follow once the principle is understood.    Fortunately modern grants of arms have tended to return to an earlier simplicity and blazons to a more straightforward wording.

An alternative blazon of the arms of the Westminster City Council, taken from 'Civic Heraldry' by C. W. Scott-Giles, is as follows:

ARMS: Azure, a gold portcullis; a gold chief charged with two Tudor roses and between them a pale containing the arms of Edward the Confessor, namely azure with a gold cross flory and five gold martlets.

CREST: On a wreath gold and azure, a portcullis sable between two roses, that on the dexter red and on the other white, each with stems and leaves proper.

SUPPORTERS: Two lions ermine each charged on the body with a gold portcullis; the dexter lion with a gold collar charged with three red roses and the other with a collar azure with three white roses, the roses having seeds and sepals proper.

MOTTO: Custodi civitatem Domine.    'Keep the City, O Lord'.

The arms of the Westminster City Council are composed of the emblems of two monarchs who are particularly associated with Westminster Abbey: Edward the Confessor, who began the rebuilding of the ancient church of St. Peter, and Henry VII who added the chapel which bears his name.    The rose and portcullis are Tudor and Beaufort badges.    The ermine lions, supporters of the arms of Cecil, were adopted in token of a family which has for centuries been associated closely with Westminster; Sir William Cecil, who became Lord Burleigh, and was Lord High Treasurer in Elizabeth I's reign, having been the City's first Lord High Steward, and his descendant, the Marquess of Salisbury, holding the same civic office in 1902 at the time the supporters were granted.

The 'trick' of the achievement in Fig. 8a was made from the blazon, also the 'trick' of the arms in Fig. 8b.    These give the information required to make the drawing in Fig. 8c.    There are certain details specially noted in the 'tricks' such as the type of ermine tails on the supporters, the number of bars on the portcullis in the arms and on the crest, and on the supporters; the number of links in each of the chains; these details are noted from the painting in the margin of the Patent, they are not specified in the blazon.    Unless the artist wishes to carry out his drawing exactly similar to the original, the alternative rendering of the arms in Fig. 8c is correct in essentials.

a. Seal of Robert Fitzwalter, 1198–1234.  *British Museum*

1b. Seal of Margaret Beauchamp, 1455, wife of John Talbot, Earl of Shrewsbury.  Suspended by their straps, from the ragged staff badge of the Earls of Warwick, are the arms of her father, Richard Beauchamp, Earl of Warwick, and the impaled arms of her husband and herself. *British Museum*

1d. Seal of William Hoo, 1427. *British Museum*

reat Seal of Edward III, 1360.  Reverse.  Note the armorials on the and on the horse trappings, also the relative proportions of shield, and crest and the vigorous movement.  *British Museum*

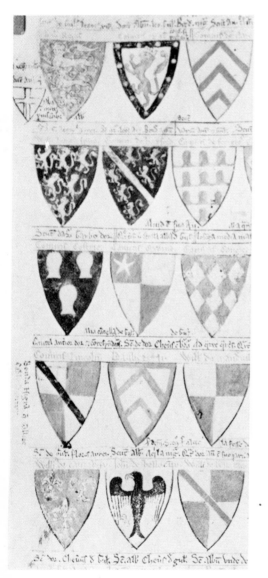

*2a*. Part of an early Roll of Arms. Matthew Paris. 13th century. *British Museum*

*2b*. Maniple, with arms embroidered in silk linen. English, early 14th century. *Victoria Albert Museum. Crown Copyright*

3. Garter stall-plate of Hugh Stafford, Lord Bourchier, *c.* 1421. The helmet, shield and crest are turned to the sinister, in order to face the high altar, as the plate is on the Gospel side of St. George's Chapel, Windsor. From 'The Stall Plates of the Knights of the Order of the Garter'. W. H. St. John Hope

4a. Arms from the chantry of Abbot Ramrydge, d. 1524, St. Albans.   An example of a rebus or allusive device: A ram gorged with a collar inscribed with the letters RYGE.   Note the curved and ridged shield and varied textures.   *Copyright F. H. Crossley, Chester*

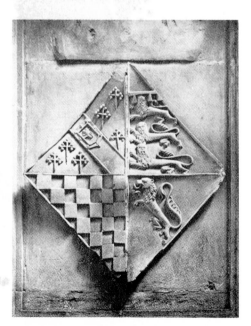

4b. Quartered arms on a lozenge. Fitzroy tomb, Framlingham Church, Suffolk. *Copyright F. H. Crossley*

4c. Shield surrounded by the Garter ensigned with a crest coronet. Fitzroy tomb, Framlingham Church, Suffolk. *Copyright F. H. Crossley*

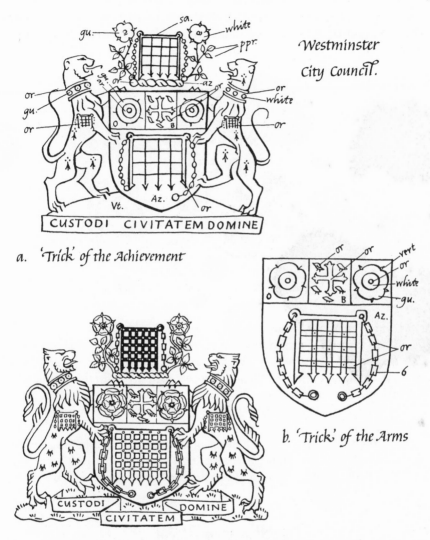

Westminster
City Council.

a. 'Trick' of the Achievement

b. 'Trick' of the Arms

c. The armorial bearings of the Westminster City Council
correct in essentials but without helm or mantling.

Fig. 8. An Achievement of Arms and its component parts

The representations of the arms of Westminster City Council displayed on their road signs, dust-carts and the like, closely resemble the illustration in Fox-Davies, 'Book of Public Arms', 1915 (Fig. 9).

Fig. 9. Arms of Westminster from the *Book of Public Arms,* Fox-Davies

It is very important for an artist to have a reliable blazon of the coat of arms in front of him before he starts to make his drawing. Whenever possible it is desirable to see the original Grant of Arms with its authentic blazon and the painting of the arms in the margin, even if he intends to depart radically from this painting in style. Unreliable source material can lead to serious errors and waste of time.

The method of designing various achievements is discussed in Part Three of this book.

The component parts of an achievement are now analysed in progressive order starting with the shield. Sufficient information is given about each heraldic feature to enable a designer to deal with most of the basic problems of design in heraldry.

## THE SHIELD. *The Shapes of Shields*

From the beginning of the development of heraldry the shield has been the principal object for the display of arms: in warfare, tournaments, architectural embellishments and seals. The shield actually bears the arms and therefore is the main part of an achievement; it may be used without any of the other devices which make up a coat of arms as a whole.

The shape and the area of the shield have influenced the design of the charges it bears. These forms of shields have changed through the centuries and the stylistic variety of their proportions and outlines gives the modern designer room for apt choice for different purposes. An adequate knowledge of historical styles is an obvious advantage to a designer. Arms do not necessarily require to be borne upon a shield, they may be equally correct when displayed on any other shape and it has become the custom for the arms of a woman to be displayed upon a lozenge (Fig. 75); when she has an insignia of an order encircling her arms, a roundel or an oval is often employed for the latter, or when her arms are being marshalled with her husband, he possessing such insignia and she not. (See pp. 113–14.)

Fig. 10. Norman horseman in mail armour with a kite-shaped shield, charging the English carrying round shields and axes, at the Battle of Hastings, 1066. Detail from the Bayeux Tapestry

Fig. 11. Norman shields with leather guiges

The long Norman shields of the 11th and 12th centuries were kite-shaped and curved horizontally to protect the body. The top was rounded or straight with rounded corners. These styles were followed by a shorter shield of almost triangular form, the curved outlines of the sides springing from the upper corners (Figs. 12a, b). Shields of this period were the first to display armorial bearings and fine examples of this equilateral style may be seen on 13th- and 14th-century seals and memorials.

During the second half of the 13th century and early 14th century the proportions changed and the shield became narrower (Figs. 12c, d). The sides began at right angles to the horizontal upper edge and thence (from a point about a quarter of the height of the shield) curved downward to the point at the base of the shield. This handsome tapering form is known as the 'heater' shape on account of its resemblance to a smoothing iron. It is a beautifully proportioned shield of which the quartered arms of the Black Prince, in Canterbury Cathedral, is an outstanding example. This shield shape which combines dignity and vigour has never lost its popularity with designers of heraldry in architecture and in the crafts.

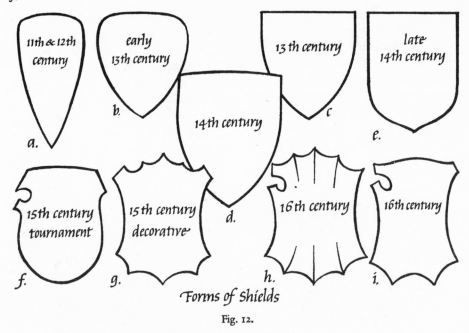

Forms of Shields

Fig. 12.

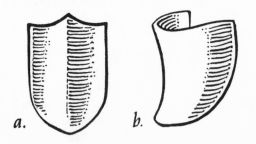

Fig. 13 *a* Prototype of the ridged Renaissance shield
*b* Shield with double curve, convex from side to side, concave from top to bottom

Towards the end of the 14th century the shield became more square in shape so as to allow room for charges in the base (Fig. 12*e*).

The forerunner of the ridged Renaissance shield had a sharp arris and rounded base, the play of light and shade on it especially when modelled in relief made it a popular shape for decorative purposes (Fig. 13*a*).

A shield used in defence was curved from side to side in order to deflect a blow, later on the base of the shield was curved upwards and subsequently the top as well, giving it a double curvature (Fig. 13*b*).

The tournament shield *à bouche* which had a semicircular hole in the side into which the shaft of the lance fitted closely, strongly influenced later forms used for ornamental purposes, in architecture particularly (Fig. 12*f*).

In the late 15th century and in Tudor times the cusped and fluted form of shield was developed which later came to resemble a cartouche more than a shield (Figs. 12*g*, *h*, *i*).

Fig. 14. Shapes of shields drawn from a set of metal templates which the author has found useful in designing achievements

The further removed the shield became from practical use, the more decorative it grew in form, and elaborate shields continued to be displayed on ceremonial occasions for some time after their use in combat had ceased.

With the invention of printing a new field opened up for the widespread use of heraldic designs. The elaborately decorative bookplates of Albrecht Dürer are examples of the art of this period with its taste for fantastic shield shapes.

A knowledge of the variety of shields will enable the designer to choose the shape most suitable for the charges to be displayed. An attenuated charge such as a rampant lion will suit a long, pointed shield; but three lions passant guardant, or three charges blazoned two and one require a wider form. A squarer type with rounded base is suited to quartered arms.

The forms of shields can be very subtle in their slight variations one from another and in the springing of their curves; which the designer will discover during the process of constructing shields geometrically (Fig. 19).

These variations in proportion can be made to serve the mood of an occasion. A shield of severe and dignified outline is appropriate for architectural decoration or for a ceremonial occasion. One of more elaborate outline or lively shape might be

From the stall-plate of Humphrey
Duke of Buckingham, 1429.

Fig. 15.

Fig. 16. Seal of Queen Margaret, 1299, which displays the arms of her husband King Edward I, surrounded with the fleurs-de-lis of her father on the field of the seal

suitable for decorating an illuminated Address of Welcome, or for the décor of a pageant.

In addition to variations of shape the designer may also choose wide variations in the tilt of the vertical axis of the shield (Fig. 15). Such a shield 'couché' is usually depicted sloping to the left, as looked at. If on the north side of a church, however, the shield would couch to the right, respecting the altar, and its charges if animate would be shown looking or moving to the right. (Plate 3. Fig. 37a.)

Fig. 17.

*a* Detail from Queen Eleanor monument, Lincoln Cathedral

*b* Detail from Queen Eleanor monument, Lincoln Cathedral

On medieval monuments and seals shields are often shown as suspended from the guige or shield-belt; they may be hung from a tree stock, a boss or a corbel; the shield may hang vertically (Figs. 16, 17a, b), or at an angle to the sinister in which case it is termed couché, and figures of angels were frequently used to hold shields, couché or vertical.

A shield of arms may be called an escutcheon, but when a shield is borne as a charge on a shield of arms it is termed an inescutcheon (Figs. 27, 105).

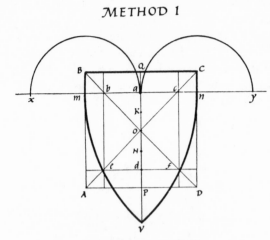

Fig. 18. How to construct a shield, METHOD I

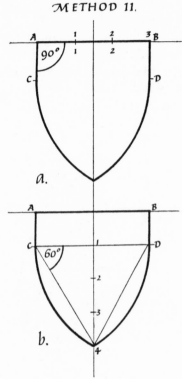

Fig. 19. How to construct a shield
a METHOD II.  A speedier method
b Alternative method of construction

## THE SHIELD. *How to construct a Shield with Instruments*

No form of shield is ideal from an artist's point of view when drawn geometrically, but the accurate use of compasses, ruler and set square is a necessary skill
for the designer of heraldry.

METHOD I (Fig. 18).  Adapted from 'The Laws of Fésole', Vol. I, by John Ruskin.
To construct a shield 2″ wide draw the square ABCD 2″ wide with the
diagonals ACBD and the vertical PQ through the centre O.  Divide OQ, OP,
each into three equal parts by the points K, a, N, d.  Through a and d draw the
level lines cutting the diagonals in b, c, e and f and produce bc cutting the sides of
the square in m and n as far towards x and y as necessary.  With centres m and n
and the equal radii ma, na, describe semicircles, cutting xy in x and y.  With
centres x and y, and the equal radii xn, ym, describe arcs nv, mv, cutting each other

and the line QP, produced in V. The precision of their concurrence will test the accuracy of construction.

METHOD II (Fig. 19a). A speedier method of constructing a shield:

The proportions are those of a typical 14th-century shield, such as that of the Black Prince in Canterbury Cathedral; it is an excellent model for general heraldic purposes.

Rule a vertical line and at right angles to it, equally on either side, measure off the width of the top of the shield to make AB.

Divide the top of the shield equally into thirds, at A and B drop lines at right-angles to AB and measure off one third for AC and BD, with the point of the compass in C and radius CD describe the arc from D to where it strikes the central vertical line, repeat the same arc with D as centre. The two curves must meet exactly on the vertical line. The line AB could equally well be divided into quarters and the resulting shape would be slightly different.

*Alternative method of construction* (Fig. 19b):

The vertical is divided into quarters and AC and BD are each the length of one quarter, the arcs described from C and D enclose an equilateral triangle.

By constructing a number of nearly similar shields of slightly varying proportions the subtle difference in their shapes will be appreciated.

# THE SHIELD. *The Field*

It is important to realise that the shield is visualized as being held in front of its bearer on the left arm, the side towards the right shoulder being the dexter side, and that towards the left shoulder the sinister side. Therefore in a painting of a shield the sinister side is on the viewer's right and the dexter side is on his left.

The heraldic convention is that all shields are considered as square in the field and are thus theoretically capable of being divided into quarters.

In Fig. 20 consider the square ABCD as the field, the honour points are seen in their correct positions and named as shown

The letters a, b, c, d, e, f, are convenient for making the Chief and Base positions. K stands for Knighthood, or honour point, N for Nombril and O for the sign of belt or girdle, thus the letters KON, in this order, are easy to remember as the first syllable of KÖNIG, the Teutonic word for King.[1]

---

[1] Adapted from the 'Laws of Fésole', Vol. 1, by John Ruskin.

*Field of the Shield*        *The honour points*

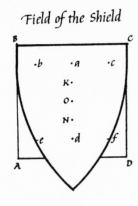

a.   *Middle Chief*

b.   *Dexter Chief*

c.   *Sinister Chief*

к.   *Honour*

o.   *Fess*

N.   *Nombril*

d.   *Middle Base*

e.   *Dexter Base*

f.   *Sinister Base*

Fig. 20. The Shield: The field.   The honour points

## THE SHIELD. *Divisions of the Field* (Fig. 21)

The field of the shield may be divided by a line or lines into two or more parts, the parts being of different colours or metals.   The divided field is described as party, or parted per pale, per fess, and so on according to the pattern.   Quarterly is a more usual term than per cross for a shield divided into four.   Gyronny is usually drawn of eight pieces, as the divisions are called.   The partition lines may be plain or ornamental.   Each division of the field of a shield is tinctured.   The first mentioned tincture is on the upper side of the dividing line; in the case of 'per pale' it is on the dexter side of the line; divided 'quarterly' the first mentioned tincture is in the top dexter, or first quarter and the bottom sinister, or fourth quarter, i.e. the same tinctures are diagonally opposite one another.   When the field of a shield is divided per saltire the first mentioned tincture is in the upper part of the shield and in the base; the second tincture in the dexter and sinister sections, opposite to one another.   In 'gyronny' each piece is tinctured alternately, the first mentioned tincture is in the piece at the top dexter of the shield between the bend and pale dividing lines.

## THE SHIELD. *Varied Fields* (Fig. 22)

Varied fields are made by further divisions which always consist of an even number of pieces, for example, barry, bendy and paly.   Crossing lines produce chequey which is a combination of paly and barry; also lozengy and fusily made by

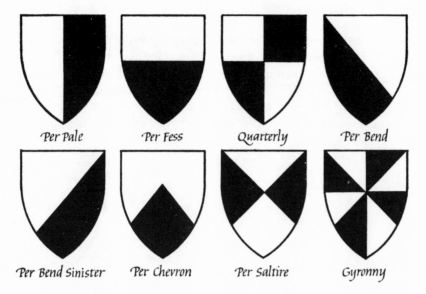

Fig. 21. The Shield: Divisions of the field

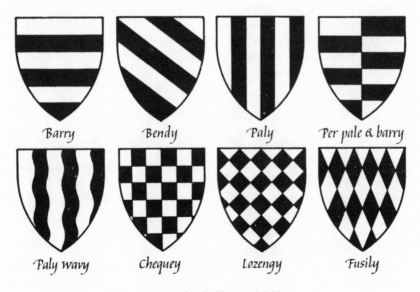

Fig. 22. The Shield: Varied fields

crossing diagonals; fusily consisting of narrower diamond shaped pieces than lozengy.

It is particularly important to realize that in the blazon of parted and varied fields the tincture first mentioned in the case of per fess, bend, chevron, saltire and barry is that of the chief or top of the shield; per pale and paly that on the dexter side; per cross and chequey that on the dexter chief corner; bendy that in the sinister chief; gyronny that in the sinister chief half of the first quarter. This enables the designer to know how to place the tinctures correctly when working from a blazon only.

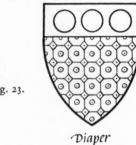

Fig. 23.

*Diaper*

# DIAPER

To enrich the plain surface of the field of a shield and in some cases that of charges, decoration may be applied; this is called diapering (Fig. 23). It need not conform to the law of tinctures and it can be executed in any colour or metal. The pattern used is purely ornamental, usually geometrical in character; it must not compete with heraldic tinctures and must not be mistaken for charges or for a powdered field. Effective diapers can be made with gold patterns on a field of any of the colours, or by painting the ornament in a different tint to that of the field.

# THE SHIELD. *Dividing Lines* (Fig. 24)

The lines dividing the shield into parts, or outlining the ordinaries, or other figures placed on the field, may be plain or ornamental. A line is plain unless it is stated otherwise in the blazon. The following are the ornamental lines in general use:

ENGRAILED (24a, b): The cusps may be of any suitable size or depth of curvature. When used as a party line they point to the dexter; in per fess and per chevron they point upwards. The points must turn outwards from an ordinary.

Fig. 24. The Shield:
　　　　Dividing lines

a. *Per pale engrailed*

b. *Fess engrailed*

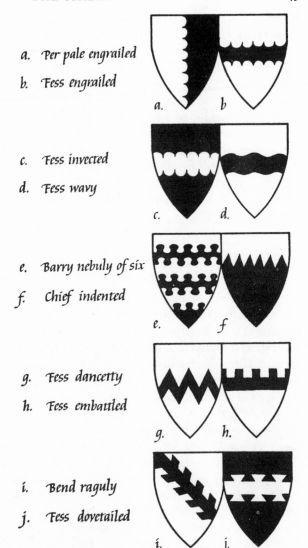

c. *Fess invected*

d. *Fess wavy*

e. *Barry nebuly of six*

f. *Chief indented*

g. *Fess dancetty*

h. *Fess embattled*

i. *Bend raguly*

j. *Fess dovetailed*

INVECTED　(24c): Invected is engrailed reversed.

WAVY　(24d) Any regular undulating line, so long as it cannot be confused with nebuly.

NEBULY　(24e): A suggestion of clouds. There are various forms.

INDENTED　(24f): Consists of a number of small serrations.

DANCETTY  (24*g*): Usually consists of outlines of three or more chevrons.

EMBATTLED  (24*h*): In the case of the fess and chevron, the crenellations are applied to the upper line only, unless blazoned embattled-counter-embattled. When applied to a chevron the sides of the crenellations are kept at right angles to the ordinary.

RAGULY  (24*i*): Similar to embattled but with sloping crenellations. When applied to a fess, pale or bend it suggests the stumps of branches and the projections on both sides of the ordinaries slope the same way and may alternate. In a cross the projections point along the limbs outwards from the centre.

DOVETAILED (24*j*): Interlocking shapes of similar size.

POTENTY  (30): From the word potence meaning a crutch.

## THE SHIELD. The Ordinaries (Fig. 25)

The simple flat bands or geometrical figures of painted colour or metal superimposed on the field of the shield are called ordinaries. These ordinaries are thought by some to arise from the structure of the original shields used in combat, which were made of leather stretched on a foundation of wood and strengthened with bands of metal. The ordinaries divide the field symmetrically and are of great importance in the satisfactory arrangement of the design; they are admirably proportioned and displayed in the earlier coats of arms.

The proportion of the ordinaries to the field varies when the ordinary is alone on the shield, or when it is between charges, or is charged itself. The width of the CHIEF, FESS and PALE should be slightly less than one-third of the shield when neither the field nor the ordinary are charged or when both are charged. The ordinaries should occupy a full third when they are charged upon a plain field.

The BEND, CHEVRON, CROSS and SALTIRE should occupy one-third if charged and one-fifth if uncharged. Charges placed on a bend slope with it unless blazoned otherwise. The chevron has its point in chief unless blazoned as the reverse; it is usually drawn as a right angle, but it may vary according to space and the type of charges upon it; it is unattractive if it is flattened out, i.e. drawn at a more obtuse angle than a right angle. A charge on the centre of a chevron is placed erect, and charges on the chevron as a whole do not generally slope with it. A PILE usually issues from the chief, but may do so from either side or the bottom of the shield. Charges on a saltire slope with the limbs unless otherwise blazoned. The crosses of St. Andrew and St. Patrick are saltires. The four arms of a saltire should be as nearly equal as possible to one another in length with the upper and lower angles slightly less than right angles.

Ordinaries may have straight border lines, or they may be varied by any of the ornamental dividing lines (Fig. 24).

The character and weight of ordinaries and other charges must be considered together when deciding their proportions and the experienced designer will place them by eye. There is no fixed rule for proportions and those given here are intended merely as a guide. The aim of the designer is the harmonious and well balanced display of all the constituent parts of the arms.

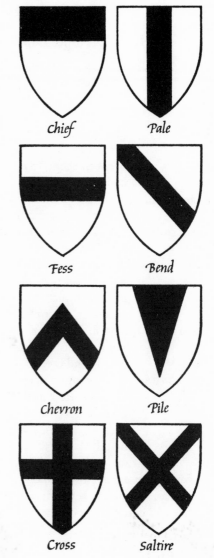

Fig. 25. The Shield: The ordinaries

*chief*  *Pale*

*Fess*  *Bend*

*Chevron*  *Pile*

*Cross*  *Saltire*

## *THE SHIELD. The Diminutives* (Fig. 26)

Ordinaries may occupy about one-third of the depth or width of a shield. Similar ordinaries are not usually repeated on one shield, that is to say two fesses, or two chevrons, but some of the ordinaries have diminutive forms especially named:

THE BAR — (26a): The bar is narrower than the fess. Two or more bars may occur together. Bars must show the field above and below and between them, to distinguish them from the varied field known as barry.

BARS GEMELLES (26b): The diminutive of the bar is the BARRULET. When placed in couples they are called BARS GEMELLES (twin bars).

FESS COTISED — (26c, d): When a barrulet is placed on either side of the fess, the fess is said to be cotised or double cotised.

PALLETS — (26e, f): Two or more palewise strips are called PALLETS and these must be distinguished from PALY, as bars are from barry. The Endorse which is narrower than a PALLET is usually found in pairs enclosing other charges, thus a pale is endorsed.

BENDLETS — (26g, h): Three or more narrow bends on a shield are BENDLETS and must be distinguished from BENDY. A bend between cotises is called bend cotised, or if there are two on each side, double cotised.

CHEVRONELS: — Two or more narrow chevrons may be borne on one shield, three or more are called CHEVRONELS. They are placed one above the other unless otherwise specified. As with the fess and bend the chevron may be cotised or double cotised, or double close as it may be called.

For a general guide the proportion of the barrulet may be a quarter of the width of the bar, the pallet, bendlet and chevronel half the width of the bar, and the endorse and cotise a quarter the width of their ordinaries.

5a. Knights jousting. Misericord, Worcester Cathedral. *National Buildings Record*

. Stuart Royal Arms and Supporters. Detail of gates in a carved wooden screen. King's College Chapel, ambridge. An interesting solution to the problem of space filling. *Crown Copyright*

6a. Arms and supporters of the foundress, Lady Margaret Beaufort, carved in wood and painted. Observe how the crest is turned at the same angle as the helm. St. John's College, Cambridge. *Crown Copyright*

6b. Carved and painted armorial panel over the main gateway, St. John's College, Cambridge, 1511. The arms of the foundress, Lady Margaret Beaufort, with yale supporters, are surrounded by a pattern of daisies, marguerites and borage and flanked by the rose and portcullis badges. The coronets are set with marguerites, pearls, crosses and fleurs-de-lis. *Crown Copyright*

The crowned arms and supporters of King Henry VII in King's College Ante Chapel, Cambridge, flanked by Tudor badges of the crowned portcullis and rose. The bold carving of heraldic detail is notable. *Crown Copyright*

Detail from the south porch of King's College Chapel, Cambridge, showing the crowned arms of Henry VII. e varying stances of the dragon and greyhound supporters within the circles should be compared with those of same supporters in the illustration above. *Crown Copyright*

8a. Panel of stained and painted glass. The arms of Calthorpe impaling Stapleton. English, about 1475. *Victoria & Albert Museum. Crown Copyright*

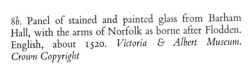

8b. Panel of stained and painted glass from Barham Hall, with the arms of Norfolk as borne after Flodden. English, about 1520. *Victoria & Albert Museum. Crown Copyright*

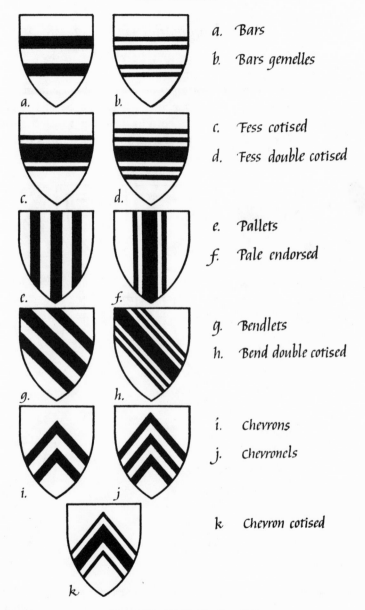

a. Bars

b. Bars gemelles

c. Fess cotised

d. Fess double cotised

e. Pallets

f. Pale endorsed

g. Bendlets

h. Bend double cotised

i. Chevrons

j. Chevronels

k Chevron cotised

Fig. 26. The Shield: The dimunitives

## THE SHIELD. The Sub-ordinaries (Figs. 27, 28, 29)

THE BORDURE: The bordure or border may be plain or made with ornamental lines, it may be parted or charged.

THE INESCUTCHEON: The inescutcheon may be borne singly or in groups and it is often charged. A single inescutcheon should be appreciably smaller than the area enclosed by a bordure in order to distinguish between them. The inescutcheon of pretence is usually smaller in proportion than a single inescutcheon borne as a charge.

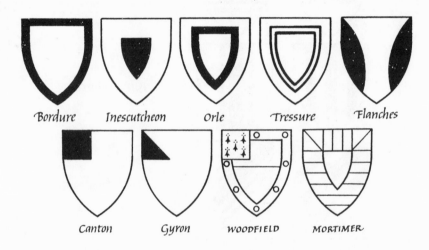

Bordure    Inescutcheon    Orle    Tressure    Flanches

Canton    Gyron    WOODFIELD    MORTIMER

Fig. 27. The Shield: The sub-ordinaries

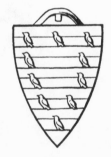

Fig. 28. Barry argent and azure, an orle of martlets gules: De Valence

THE ORLE: The orle is an inescutcheon with the centre cut out leaving only a narrow border. Charges placed along the line an orle would occupy are said to be 'in orle' (Fig. 28), *Barry argent and azure, an orle of martlets gules:* de Valence.

THE TRESSURE: The tressure is a narrow border inside the edge of the shield, usually double and enriched with fleurs-de-lis and sometimes with other devices. The space between the double tressure is voided.

FLANCHES: Flanches are always in pairs; they consist of curved lines from the top corners of the shield to the sinister base.

THE CANTON: The canton is a small rectangle in the dexter chief occupying less than one quarter of the shield—it is frequently charged. The earliest form of the canton is the quarter. When a canton is borne with a bordure the bordure stops where it touches both, being on the same plane, unless the bordure has been added later as a difference. Blazon: *Per fess gules and argent, a bordure gold charged with eight torteaux, over all a canton ermine:* Woodfield.

GYRON: A gyron is the lower half of a canton or quarter which has been divided by a diagonal line from the dexter or sinister chief. Blazon: *Barry gold and azure with the chief paly and the corners gyronny with a silver scutcheon:* Mortimer.

THE LOZENGE (29*a*): The lozenge is diamond shaped.

THE FUSIL (29*b*): The fusil is a similar but narrower shape.

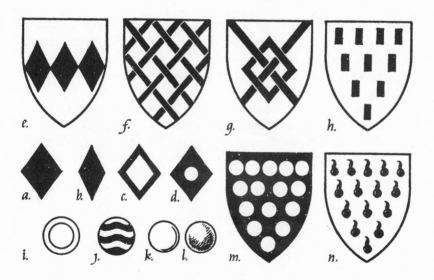

Fig. 29. The Shield: The Sub-Ordinaries. *a* Lozenge. *b* Fusil. *c* Mascle. *d* Rustre. *e* Lozenges conjoined in fess. *f* Fretty. *g* The fret. *h* Semy with billets. *i* Annulet. *j* Heraldic fountain. *k, l, m.* Roundles or roundels: *k* A flat object. *l* A round object. *m* Semy of bezants. *n* Goutty de poix

THE MASCLE (29c): The mascle is a voided lozenge.

THE RUSTRE (29d): The rustre is a lozenge pierced with a round hole, but its in-frequency scarcely justifies its inclusion as a sub-ordinary. Lozenges and fusils may be conjoined in fess, bend or cross (29e).

FRETTY (29f): Consists of bendlets, dexter and sinister, interlaced; they cover the whole field.

THE FRET (29g): The fret is one bendlet dexter and one sinister interlaced with a mascle.

A BILLET (29h): A billet is an upright oblong figure. A field semée, semy, or sown with billets is billety.

ANNULET (29i): An annulet is a plain ring, it may appear singly or in groups.

ROUNDLES or
ROUNDELS (29j–m): These are circular objects, their names and tinctures are:

| | | |
|---|---|---|
| Bezant. | Derived from a Byzantine coin. | Or. |
| Plate. | From Plata, silver. | Argent. |
| Hurt. | Derived from Hurtleberry. | Azure. |
| Torteau. | A cake. | Gules. |
| Pellet. | A cannon shot. | Sable. |
| Pomme. | An apple. | Vert. |

A roundle barry wavy argent and azure is an heraldic fountain. The coin is painted as a flat object, the others as round. A field scattered, or semy with roundles is termed semy of bezants, or bezanty, semy of plates or platy, and so on. E.g. *Sable, fifteen bezants or* for DUCHY of Cornwall (Fig. 29m).

Similar to semy is goutée or goutty, in which the field is covered with drops, these have different names according to their tinctures: Goutty d'or—gold; Goutty d'eau—argent; Goutty de sang—gules; Goutty de l'armes—azure; Goutty de olive—vert; Goutty de poix—sable.

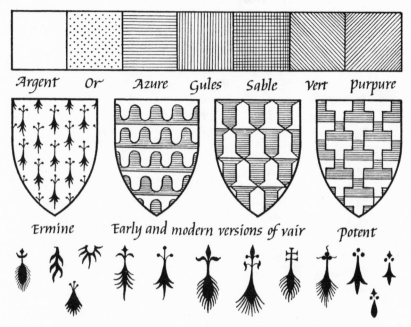

Argent    Or    Azure    Gules    Sable    Vert    Purpure

Ermine        Early and modern versions of vair        Potent

Early and modern versions of ermine-tails

Fig. 30. Heraldic Tinctures

# HERALDIC TINCTURES

In the Middle Ages arms on shields were simple in design and bold in their colours. The choice of colour was of practical importance, the aim was to make the arms clearly visible at a distance for purposes of identification in combat.

In heraldic usage there are two metals, five colours and two groups of furs. The metals, colours and furs together are termed tinctures. The metals, which are gold and silver, are often represented by yellow and white. The colours are red, blue, black, green and purple, there are other tinctures, but they are rarely seen in English heraldry. Objects represented in their natural colours are blazoned proper, contrasting colours are visible from a greater distance than colours that are similar and for this reason it became a general principle not to place a metal on a metal, or a colour on a colour. There are exceptions to this rule; a party field of metal and colour can have placed upon it a charge of another metal, or colour, provided the charge rests on the field as a whole; the rule does not apply to bordures; or to a charge which surmounts both the field and another charge.

The following table gives the heraldic names of the tinctures, their abbreviations and the way they may be indicated by hatching (Fig. 30).

| TINCTURE | HERALDIC NAME | ABBREVIATION |
|---|---|---|
| *Metals:* | | |
| Gold, yellow | Or | O. |
| Silver, white | Argent | Arg. |
| *Colours:* | | |
| Blue | Azure | Az. |
| Red | Gules | Gu. |
| Black | Sable | Sa. |
| Green | Vert | Vt. |
| Purple | Purpure | Purp. |
| Charges represented in their natural colours are blazoned | Proper | Ppr. |
| *Furs:* | | |
| Ermine: | Black tails on white ground | |
| Ermines: | White tails on black ground | |
| Erminois: | Black tails on gold ground | |
| Pean: | Gold tails on black ground | |
| Vair ⎫ Potent ⎭ | Represented by alternate pieces coloured white and blue unless otherwise stated. | |

Hatching is a convention which derived from the use of engraving in the 17th century. It is not attractive artistically, but it is useful as a kind of shorthand to indicate tinctures in black and white (Fig. 6). Argent is represented by leaving the surface white; gold by scattering it with black dots; azure by drawing horizontal black lines across it; gules by vertical black lines; sable is represented by cross-hatching; vert by diagonal lines to the dexter, and purpure by diagonal lines to the sinister. The two colours most easily confused in this system are red and blue, a mnemonic is the word horizon=horizontal lines=blue. A more convenient method for quick reporting is 'tricking' where the abbreviations are used instead of hatching lines to indicate tinctures (Fig 8).

In heraldic painting the metal gold may be represented by pure gold powder or gold leaf. Pure gold is costly but it does not tarnish and it will take a low or high burnish depending on the way it is applied and treated. Yellow pigment may be used for the metal. When an animal which is naturally yellow is blazoned proper it must obviously be painted yellow and not gold.

White paint is generally substituted for silver in representing the metal. White paint mixed with a very little black makes a satisfactory silvery grey, which for most purposes adequately represents the metal. Silver, or white gold, should not be used as it will quickly turn black unless varnished. It is better to use aluminium powder and aluminium leaf, although neither of these will take a burnish. Platinum leaf which is thicker and stiffer than gold leaf and therefore more difficult to apply, will take and retain a high burnish and will not tarnish.

In heraldic design simplicity of colouring is the aim. The primary colours, red, blue, yellow, black and white, are most generally used. The secondary colours green and purple are comparatively rare. Heraldic colours should be flat in tone, strong in colour, with a definite outline. The metals, colours and furs stated in the blazon must be strictly followed in the painting, but there is no rule as to their depth of tone, or the degree of modelling or finish, the choice here depends on the purpose for which the design is made and the inclination of the artist.

The furs are divided into two groups called Ermine and Vair (Fig. 30). Ermine actually consists of many small furs sewn together; heraldically the black tipped tails make a regular pattern: these tails are represented in a conventional form which has many variants.

Vair represents, also in a conventional form, the skins of squirrels, the pieces are alternately blue and white, blue from the back and white from the belly of the animal. The pieces may be rounded or angular in form. Certain styles have been given distinct names, e.g. Potent, from potence, a crutch, but all the furs in this group are represented by white and blue pieces unless otherwise specified in the blazon.

A good basic principle in choosing the colours for heraldic painting is that they should be as strong and true as possible, the reds neither too orange nor too purplish, and the blues neither as hot as French ultramarine nor as green as Prussian blue. In heraldry red should be clear and bright, not crimson, pink, or terra-cotta; vermilion and scarlet vermilion are the best red pigments in both oils and water-colours. Purplish blues should be avoided. Ultramarine blue with a little viridian or cerulean added is a good water-colour mixture. Oil colours, being stronger than water-colours, can be modified with admixtures without losing force.

Where there is a party field of red and blue the tones of these two colours should be near together for the sake of unity.

Charges will be more clearly differentiated if the tone of the colour or metal is positively lighter or darker than the tone of the field. A strong outline is commonly used to define the shapes of the charges but a skilful use of tone will enable the designer to dispense with the outline if he prefers.

In representing the metal gold both yellow ochre and raw sienna are more sympathetic and realistic than the vivid lemon or cadmium yellows, but there is sufficient scope in representing this metal for imaginative variations.

The colour green is uncommon in heraldry. It can be represented by viridian in water-colour or opaque oxide of chromium in water-colour and oil. Viridian in water-colour being transparent requires the addition of lemon yellow, or aureolin and Chinese white to give it sufficient body. Opaque oxide of chromium may need the addition of a little viridian or yellow ochre according to the tone required. Emerald green pigment should not only be avoided on aesthetic grounds but also because it may cause discolouring when associated with vermilion and French ultramarine.

The black pigments commonly used are ivory and lamp blacks. Black harmonizes with the other colours in the blazon better if it is greyed down very slightly by adding a small quantity of white pigment; this greying enables the artist to use a full strength black outline or modelling if required.

A mixture of blue and red is better for purple, rather than the use of the purple aniline paints which are sold in water-colours and oils.

Colours in heraldic painting should usually be opaque and those that are not naturally opaque should be mixed with a little white to give them body. The best quality pigments should always be used for commissioned work that is intended to last.

Winsor and Newton colours on their Selected List are considered permanent.

Work to be shown out of doors naturally requires weather-proof pigments and varnish; advice from the paint manufacturers about their application is valuable.

## CHARGES

A shield is said to be charged with the devices upon it, although the term usually applies to objects other than the ordinaries; the field of the shield and the ordinaries may themselves be charged. Charges may be used singly or in numbers.

Anything that can be depicted in form and tincture may be used as a charge and the variety is so great that only those which have a distinctive heraldic character, and are therefore of special interest to the artist, can be dealt with here.

In the early stages of heraldry as a system, the prime rules governing the choice of charges are not entirely clear, although feudal connection or dependence must have had a part to play. Care was taken, through a kind of natural sense of fitness, that one man's arms differed sufficiently from those of another. To identify was the object, but apart from this the choice of devices appears to have been arbitrary. The canting coat, or pun upon the bearer's name, was a favourite choice; *Argent three cocks gules*—Cockfield, and *Sable a fesse engrailed and three whelk shells or*— Shelley, also Applegarth (Fig. 46) and Hornby (Fig. 106).

## The Arrangement and Placing of Charges

During the 14th and 15th centuries the artistic excellence of English heraldic design was at its zenith. The craftsmen of the time had a natural eye for proportion in disposing the charges on the area of the shield, roundel, lozenge or banner; a proper balance was maintained between the field and the charges and their tinctures.

The scale of the charges in relation to the field is a matter of judgement, developed by the study of good examples. A single charge for example should comfortably fill the area of whatever shape is chosen. If it is drawn too large it will look cramped and too small a single charge will look mean. The space covered by the charges should be rather less than the area of the field which remains visible.

The disposition of plural charges is indicated in the blazon and these must be correctly placed. Three similar charges are usually blazoned two and one which is the obvious arrangement for a triangular area. When there are more than three charges their disposition should be specified in the blazon: e.g. ten bezants four three two and one. Counting reads from the chief to the base. Particularly when animals or monsters are the charges no harm is done, indeed the effect is enhanced, if they vary in size and outline (Fig. 31a).

The placing of charges may be indicated by the direction of the ordinaries, thus objects in an horizontal line across the middle of the field are said to be in fess, across the top to be in chief, one above another to be in pale and so on. This does not mean that the charges must occupy the space of a pale, bend or fess, but that they are disposed in that direction. When a fess or chevron is between three charges they are placed two above in chief and one below in base. When similar charges number more than three they are placed in groups, e.g. *Gules a bend between six cross-crosslets fitchy argent*, for Howard. *Argent a chevron gules between nine cloves sable*—Worshipful Company of Grocers (Fig. 31b and c).

The term semée, semy, sown with or powdered, is used to describe an indeterminate number of small objects equally distributed over the surface of the field (Fig. 29n), ordinary or charge.

The early method of representing a field equally distributed with small charges was to assume that the area of the shield was cut out from a larger surface of the

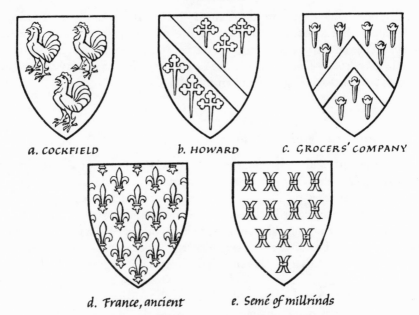

a. COCKFIELD                b. HOWARD                c. GROCERS' COMPANY

d. France, ancient              e. Semé of millrinds

Fig. 31. Charges: The arrangement and placing of charges

material and the outline therefore cut through some of the charges (Fig. 31*d*). The method often used now is to arrange the charges so that they are evenly distributed but do not touch the edge of the shield (Figs. 31*e*, 29*h*).

For convenience charges have been divided into groups.

    1.   Divine and Human Beings
    2.   The lion and other animals
    3.   Birds
    4.   Monsters
    5.   Natural objects
    6.   Inanimate objects
    7.   The Cross

In each group a few typical examples have been illustrated and their blazons given in the following pages.

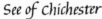 See of Salisbury

Fig. 32.

## Divine and Human Beings

Representations of Divine Beings occur in heraldry. For example the arms of the See of Chichester (Fig. 32): *Azure, a representation of our Saviour seated crowned and a glory round His head, His right hand raised in benediction, His left resting on an open book or, in His mouth a sword fessewise point to the sinister gules.* The Virgin and Child are represented in the arms of the See of Salisbury (Fig. 32): *Azure, the Holy Virgin standing crowned carrying on her right arm the Infant Christ and holding in her left hand a sceptre.* Angels appear as supporters in the arms of the Worshipful Company of Tallow Chandlers: *On either side on a mount vert an angel vested, winged and crowned with stars or.*

The saints are usually represented by their emblems such as the eagle of St. John the Evangelist, the winged lion of St. Mark, a sword for St. Paul, keys for St. Peter, the gridiron of St. Lawrence and a wheel for St. Catherine.

The blazon ought clearly to indicate the attitude and costume of human beings used in armorial bearings. For example the supporters of the Worshipful Company of Framework Knitters (Fig. 33) are: *On the dexter side a student of the University of Cambridge in academical costume of the Seventeenth Century proper and on the sinister side a female figure also in Seventeenth-Century costume habited azure, cuffs, cap, neckerchief and apron argent, holding in the dexter hand a knitting needle proper and in the sinister hand a like needle and a piece of worsted knit gules.*

The Worshipful Company of
FRAMEWORK KNITTERS

Fig. 33.

Men in armour and men in different specified uniforms and dress also figure in armorial bearings (Fig. 34).

Human beings may be couped, or cut at the waist or shoulders. The crest of the Worshipful Company of Joiners is: *a demi-man carnation* (flesh-coloured), *with a laurel garland vert about his head and waist holding with his dexter hand a lance or at rest upon his shoulder*. Parts of the human body are more usual as charges and crests than whole figures. When the human head appears as a crest or charge the type must be specified in the blazon; such as Negro, Savage, Saracen, Maiden or Child. A head is termed profile for side facing, affronty for front facing, couped or erased at the neck or shoulders. It may be wreathed, helmed or crowned. If the tincture of the hair is given the head will be said to be crined of the tincture.

An arm (Fig. 35) may be erased or couped at the elbow or shoulder; or embowed if it is bent at the elbow. It may be habited, vested and cuffed; or vambraced if in armour, the tinctures being stated. A cubit arm is couped between elbow and wrist.

The hand will be described as dexter or sinister; appaumy when it is open and showing the palm; closed; grasping an object. Any of these may be described as erect or as fesswise. A hand grasping an object or holding a tool should be drawn with care to ensure that it is holding the object correctly. (Fig. 52a.)

Legs may be couped at thigh or knee and flexed, which is bent at the knee (Fig. 35).

JOINERS' COMPANY

MERCERS' COMPANY

BARON CLONCURRY

ANNESLEY

FLETCHERS' COMPANY

Fig. 34. Crests

Worshipful Company of Joiners: On a wreath or and azure a demi-man carnation, with a laurel garland vert about his head and waist, holding with his dexter hand a lance or at rest upon his shoulder

Worshipful Company of Mercers: On a wreath of the colours issuant from a bank of clouds proper a figure of the Virgin as in the arms

Baron Cloncurry: Out of a ducal coronet or, a demi-man in armour profile, vizor closed holding in his dexter hand a sword all proper, the helmet adorned with feathers the exterior two gules the centre one argent

Annesley: A moor's head couped at the shoulders in profile proper wreathed about the temples argent and azure

The Worshipful Company of Fletchers: On a wreath or and sable an angel proper vesture and wings endorsed or feathered of many colours holding with both hands a bundle of arrows also or, headed and feathered argent encircled with a band sable

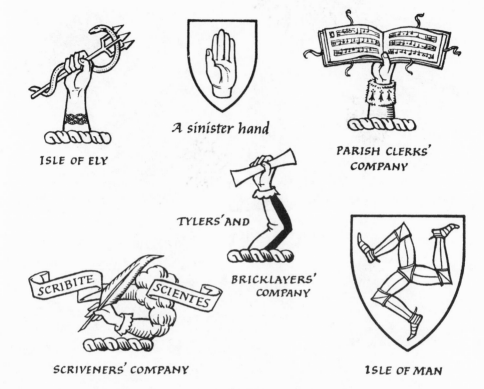

ISLE OF ELY

A sinister hand

PARISH CLERKS'
COMPANY

TYLERS' AND

BRICKLAYERS'
COMPANY

SCRIVENERS' COMPANY

ISLE OF MAN

Fig. 35.

Former Isle of Ely County Council.  Crest: On a wreath argent and azure, a human arm, the wrist charged with the Wake knot, the hand grasping a gold trident entwined with an eel proper

A hand sinister.  Baronets bear as an augmentation on their shields an escutcheon argent charged with a sinister hand gules, the Badge of Ulster

The Worshipful Company of Parish Clerks: Crest: On a wreath gules and azure a cubit arm vested azure cuffed ermine holding an open "prick-song book" all proper

The Worshipful Company of Tylers and Bricklayers.  Crest: On a wreath or and azure a dexter arm embowed vested party per pale or and gules, cuffed argent, holding in the hand proper a brick-axe or

The Worshipful Company of Scriveners.  Crest: On a wreath or and azure a dexter hand proper, holding a pen argent, the sleeve or turned up argent, issuing from a cloud proper; over all a scroll bearing the motto *Scribite scientes*

Isle of Man.  Gules three human legs in armour proper conjoined in the fesse-point at the upper part of the thighs and flexed in a triangle

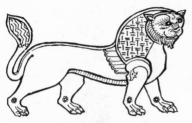

Fig. 36a Lion, from a silk, Constantinople
976–1025

Fig. 36b Lion, from an Assyrian bas-relief

Fig. 36c Lion, detail from a MS. written in the Benedictine Abbey of Moissac, c. 1070

## The Lion

The noble lion, symbol of courage and power assumed a characteristic heraldic form in the middle of the 13th century.   The oriental feeling is thought to have been derived from textiles brought to Britain from Sicily.   Whatever the sources of their inspiration the medieval craftsmen devised a beast of unmistakable vigour and great decorative value.   The attenuated heraldic lion was delineated in a simplified form, clearly recognizable at a distance.

In the 13th- and 14th-century examples of heraldic craft the placing of the lions and their proportions in relation to the space to be filled are particularly satisfying.

The drawings in Fig. 38 have been made from a variety of sources to show the types and characteristics of medieval lions rampant and lions passant guardant.   At their best these early examples admirably express the leonine vigour and ferocity of the heraldic animal.

Until about the middle of the 13th century the lion rampant was placed upright on the shield, the left forepaw is horizontal, the right forepaw and the right hindpaw rise obliquely upwards, the left hindpaw is placed firmly in the point at the base of the shield, see Figs 38a, b and d; the skeleton sketches in Fig. 39a, b and c show the

Fig. 37.

*a* Lion rampant queue fourchée in the          *b* Lion from a book of arms
arms of Sir Bermond Armand de Preissac,          painted about 1470
from the Garter stall-plate, *c.* 1421

angular, upright and abstract qualities of these lions.   The paws consisted of three
knobs like a trefoil, sometimes showing claws, the jaws might be closed or slightly
open, the tongue was not visible.   In the 14th century the right hindpaw extends
at a right angle with the left as in Fig. 38*d.*

After 1350 and during the 15th century, the attitude gradually changes so that
the lion's head is thrown back, his jaws are wide open and the tongue is visible, his
breast rises, the right hind leg has dropped and the left is bent at an angle, the right
forepaw is thrust out in an oblique line to the body as in Fig. 38*g,* the sketch in
Fig. 39*d* shows the tilt of the body expressing movement.   At this period the toes
are lengthened and often widely separated, the claws are extended and a fourth toe
has appeared.   The tail carries flame-like locks of hair.

The shield of John of Eltham, younger brother of Edward III, in Westminster
Abbey, is a splendid example of the sculptured heraldic art of the noblest period.
The lithe elasticity of the lions passant guardant (at that time termed leopards) with
their attenuated forms are intricately interlaced to fill the space on the shield.
(Fig. 38*e*).

9. Enamelled brass firedog, one of a pair, bearing the Royal Arms of the Stuarts. Second half of the 17th century. *Victoria & Albert Museum. Crown Copyright*

10a. Angel with portcullis. Boss, St. George's Chapel, Windsor. *National Buildings Record*

10b. St. George's Cross, supported by angels. Boss, George's Chapel, Windsor. *National Buildings Record*

10c. Arms of Edward the Confessor supported by angels. Boss, St. George's Chapel, Windsor. The angels holding these shields may symbolize angelic protection, they are not heraldic supporters. *National Buildings Record*

10d. Arms of France and England, ensigned with the R Crown and supported by the Red Dragon and White G hound. Roof-boss, St. George's Chapel, Windsor. *Nat Buildings Record*

11. Detail from the Grant of Arms to the Worshipful Company of Tallow Chandlers, 1456. Compare the style and balance and proportion of the armorial bearings with the Garter stall-plate on Plate 3. The illuminated initial depicts a herald in his tabard. *From 'The Armorial Bearings of the Guilds of London' by courtesy of the publishers, Frederick Warne & Co.*

a                 b

12a. Bishop Gardiner monument, Lincoln Cathedral. The arms of the bishop on the sinister are impaled with those of the See of Lincoln on the dexter. The shield is ensigned with the mitre and the keys of St. Peter are in saltire behind it. *National Buildings Record*

12b. Arms of Gervase Scrope, bearing those of Lister in an escutcheon of pretence. Monument, Lincoln Cathedral. Heraldic design is admirably expressed in low relief in slate and stone. *National Buildings Record*

12c. Arms of Scott, Earl of Deloraine, impaling those of Lister. Monument, Lincoln Cathedral. *National Buildings Record*

c

a. 1209-1265     b. 1209-1272     c.          1255

d. 1301                              f. 14th. century

e. 1316-1336

g. 1391

h. c.1421                              i. 1444

Fig. 38 a 1209–1265, Simon de Montfort, Earl of Leicester. Stone carving in Westminster Abbey. b 1209–1272, Richard, Earl of Cornwall. Stone carving in Westminster Abbey. c. 1255, Lions of England. Tile from the Chapter House, Westminster Abbey. d 1301, Shield from the seal of Henry Percy from the Baron's Letter. e 1316–1336, John of Eltham, Earl of Cornwall. Stone sculpture, St. Edmund's Chapel, Westminster Abbey. f 14th-century shield in stained glass with the arms of Mowbray, in the Victoria and Albert Museum. g 1391, Lion with forked tail from a brass at Spilsby, Lincs. h 1421, Stall-plate of Sir Simon de Felbrigg, St. George's Chapel, Windsor. i 1444, Shield from a brass at Stanford Dingley, Berks

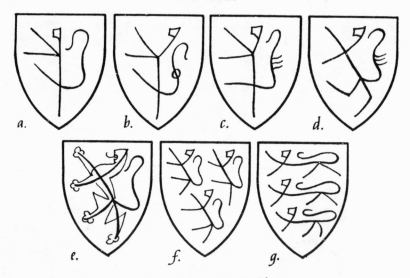

*Placing lions on the shield.*

Fig. 39.

## The Heraldic Attitudes of Animals

The attitudes of animals are heraldically important and must be carefully observed. A skeleton sketch such as those in Fig. 39e, f and g can help in placing and blocking-in animals in such a way that they fill the space and at the same time make a pattern from the living creature.

The various attitudes taken by the bodies and limbs of heraldic animals may be demonstrated by the lion (Fig. 40). The body is turned to the dexter unless otherwise specified. The positions are termed:

RAMPANT: When the body is erect, the head facing forward (i.e. sideways to the spectator) the left hind paw on the ground, the other three raised and the tail is erect.

SALIENT: In the act of springing or leaping, a variant of the lion rampant, usually both hind paws on the ground and both fore paws raised.

STATANT: Standing with all four paws on the ground, the head facing forward, tail curved over the back.

PASSANT: Walking, the dexter fore paw raised, the other three paws on the ground, head facing forward, tail curved over the back.

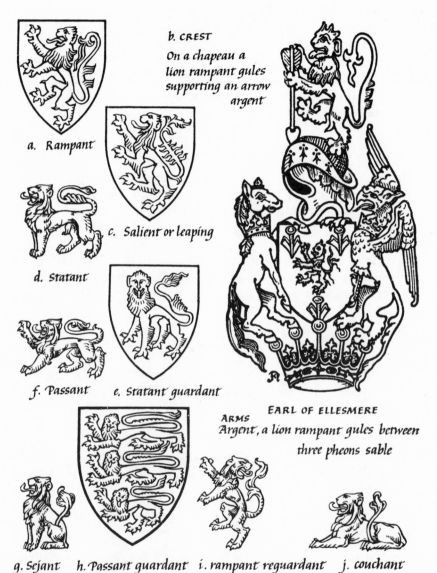

a. Rampant

b. CREST

On a chapeau a
lion rampant gules
supporting an arrow
argent

c. Salient or leaping

d. Statant

f. Passant    e. Statant guardant

ARMS    EARL OF ELLESMERE
Argent, a lion rampant gules between
three pheons sable

g. Sejant    h. Passant guardant    i. rampant reguardant    j. couchant

Fig. 40. These illustrations show the heraldic attitudes of animals. Although the style of the
drawing varies with the artist the attitudes remain heraldically correct. *a, c, e* after W. H. St.
John Hope. *b* J. Forbes Nixon. *d, f, g, i, j* after G. W. Eve, *h* after E. E. Dorling. The supporters in the arms of the Earl of Ellesmere are: dexter, a horse argent ducally gorged or;
Sinister, a griffin or, ducally gorged azure

SEJANT: Seated with forepaws on the ground, facing forward, tail passed between the hind legs and the tip of it erect.

SEJANT ERECT: Similar to sejant but with the fore paws raised.

COUCHANT: Crouching with legs and belly on the ground, facing forward, tail between the hind legs and tip erect.

DORMANT: Similar to couchant but with the head lowered on the forepaws and tail on the ground.

GUARDANT and REGUARDANT

In all the positions mentioned above the head is facing forward; these attitudes, with the exception of Dormant, are however, subject to a second variation—the head may be turned so as to face the spectator in which case the attitude is termed guardant, e.g. Statant Guardant, as in the Royal crest; Rampant Guardant, as in the dexter supporter of the Royal Arms; Passant Guardant, as in the Royal Arms of England (Fig. 107).

When the head is turned to look backwards over the shoulder the attitude nowadays is termed Reguardant, as in Fig 40.   It should be emphasized that the body of a lion, or any animal, is rampant, passant, etc., to the dexter, whichever way the head may be facing, unless it is specified otherwise.

VARIANTS.   A lion may be doubletailed, or queue fourchée (Fig. 37, 38a, g).

Two lions rampant facing one another are combatant.

Two lions rampant back to back are addorsed.   A lion is usually armed and langued gules, i.e. having red claws and a red tongue, but if gules itself, or on a field gules, it will be armed and langued azure, or any other tincture specified in the blazon.

The lion is sometimes crowned; he may be collared possibly with a chain attached to it; or he may be gorged, encircled about the throat, with a coronet.

## Parts of Animals (Fig. 41)

When a separate part of an animal is used as a charge or crest the method of its severance from the body must be correctly indicated according to the blazon.

A demi-lion is usually rampant; in this form it is more often found as a crest than a charge; the animal is severed at the loins and the tail is usually shown.

a. Demi-lion rampant   b. Lion's face   c. Jessant-de-lys   d. Lion's head erased.   e. Lion's jambe

f. Buck's head caboshed   g. Stag's head erased   h. Boar's head couped close   i. Boar's head couped at the neck.

j. Horse's head couped   k. Goat's head erased   l. Talbot's head erased

Fig. 41. Charges: Parts of animals

The lion's face is always affronty, including the beard but not the neck. Sometimes the face has a fleur-de-lis thrust through the mouth and appearing at the top of the head when it is said to be jessant-de-lis.

The head in profile, with part of the neck, may be couped or erased. Couped is represented by a clean cut, i.e. a straight line through the neck, body or limb.   Erased or torn away, by jagged points or tongues, usually three in number but this is not a rule.

The lion's jamb, gamb, i.e. the entire leg, may be a charge, and also the paw couped or erased at or below the middle joint.
The tail may appear as a charge.

## Deer and other animals

The attitudes of other animals follow those of the lion, but in some cases the positions have different names for different creatures, this particularly applies to the Deer.

The attitudes of deer, symbol of swiftness and the chase, have special terms borrowed from hunting. The stag or hart, which are heraldically the same, is at gaze when his head is affronty, springing when in the salient attitude, trippant when walking, at speed when running, and lodged when couchant or resting on the ground.

A stag is attired with his antlers which are called attires; other horned animals are armed with their horns.

A buck differs from a stag only in having broad, flat antlers. A hind has no antlers.

The antelope, reindeer, elk and other similar animals are represented as true to nature.

The head of a stag or similar animal is said to be caboshed when it is full faced with no neck.

The head of a boar may be couped or erased in two forms, at the base of the neck, English fashion, or erased close, directly behind the ears with no part of the neck being shown, Scottish fashion. When it is necessary to specify these parts of the body animals are said to be langued, of the tongue, armed, of horns, tusks and claws, and unguled or hooved.

Horses and other maned animals are said to be crined of their manes.

Hounds in heraldry are usually the talbot or greyhound.

## Monsters (Figs. 42, 43)

Heraldic monsters are creatures of classical and medieval mythology and imagination. They adopt the attitudes of other animals in heraldry such as rampant, statant and passant. They have the following characteristics:

UNICORN: The unicorn has the head and body of a horse, cloven hooves, tufted hocks, a beard and a lion's tail. A long twisted horn projects from the centre of its forehead.

42a Greek griffin from Olympia. 7th century B.C.

DRAGON: A scaly serpent-like monster with a horny head and forked tongue. It has rolls like armour on the inside of its chest and belly, a pointed tail, four legs ending in talons and a pair of bat-like wings.

WYVERN: a form of dragon with two legs only. If it is blazoned proper the head, back and legs are green, the chest, belly and insides of the wings are red.

GRIFFIN or GRYPHON: The head, breast, fore-claws and wings are those of an eagle, the body, hind legs and tail are those of a lion. It has pointed ears which distinguish it from the eagle when the head is erased, and also tufts on its lower beak. A griffin in a rampant position may be termed segreant. Without wings and with rays issuing from various parts of its body it is termed a male griffin.

HERALDIC TIGER or TYGRE: The heraldic tiger, as distinct from the tiger in its natural state, resembles a lion with a down-curving horn protruding from its nose—it has tusks in the lower jaw.

HERALDIC ANTELOPE: The heraldic antelope is closely related to the heraldic tiger; it has a lion's body and tail, the serrated horns of an antelope or ibex and the legs and hooves of a deer.

OPINICUS: The opinicus has the head, neck and wings of a griffin, the body and legs of a lion and the tail of a bear.

YALE: The yale varies in appearance, its body may be that of an antelope or goat, with the head of an antelope and the snout and tushes of a boar. Its chief characteristic is a pair of long horns, one of which points forward, the other back, and its reputed ability to swivel them around at will.

ENFIELD: The enfield has the head and ears of a fox, the body, hind legs and tail of a wolf and the forelegs and talons of an eagle.

COCKATRICE: The cockatrice is similar to a wyvern but has the head, comb, wattles and feet of a cock.

PEGASUS: Pegasus is the winged horse of classical mythology.

PELICAN IN ITS PIETY: The pelican is depicted with an eagle's head as wounding or vulning itself to feed its young with its blood.

PHOENIX: The phoenix is an eagle with a tufted crest on its head; it is always shown on its pyre and rising from the flames.

SALAMANDER: A lizard-like creature creeping amid flames.

HERALDIC SEA-LION: There are a number of sea monsters in heraldry which are half animal and half fish. The heraldic sea-lion has the head, mane and shoulders of a lion, its forelegs end in fins, the body is joined at the loins to the tail of a fish and the back is finned.

HERALDIC SEA-HORSE: An heraldic sea-horse has a horse's head and shoulders joined at the loins to a scaly fish's tail, its forelegs end in fins and pointed fins may run down its spine.

MERMAID: A mermaid has the head and body of a nude woman joined at the waist to a fish's tail. She is usually depicted combing her long hair and holding in the other hand a mirror.

MERMAN or TRITON: A merman has the head and body of a man joined at the waist to the tail of a fish.

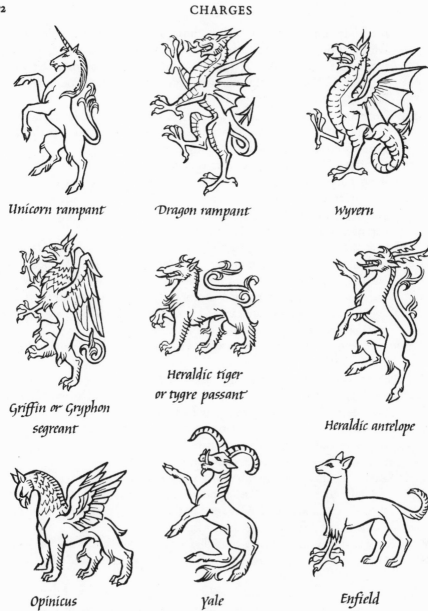

Unicorn rampant        Dragon rampant            Wyvern

Griffin or Gryphon
segreant

Heraldic tiger
or tygre passant

Heraldic antelope

Opinicus                    Yale                    Enfield

Fig. 42. Charges: Monsters

Cockatrice

Pegasus

Pelican in her piety

Phoenix

Salamander

Sea-lion

Mermaid

Merman

Sea-horse

Fig. 43. Charges: Monsters

# Birds (Fig. 44)

Many kinds of birds are found in heraldry, some of them being represented in a stylized form and others according to nature.

The eagle, symbol of victory and imperial power, early acquired a distinctive heraldic form, with an attenuated body and the feathers of the wings spread wide. An eagle displayed in this way has the body affronty, and it is either double-headed or the head is turned to one side, usually to the dexter. The wings and legs are spread out on either side, with the wing tips pointing upwards, or the wings may be inverted with the tips pointing downwards. An eagle displayed is strikingly adapted in attitude to the shield shape.

Birds may be crowned, gorged with a coronet or collar and charged on the body and wings. They may grasp an object in their beaks and talons. The heads of eagles, either couped or erased, are found as charges, also wings, and legs usually erased at the thigh.

When the beaks and legs of birds are of a different tincture to the body the bird is said to be beaked and membered of the tincture; in the case of birds of prey the term beaked and armed may be used.

The descriptive terms for the attitudes of birds generally are:

DISPLAYED: described above.

CLOSE: when standing on the ground in profile with the wings folded.

RISING: when in the same position with the wings raised.

The wings may be elevated and displayed when they are spread upwards on either side of the body. Displayed and inverted when the wings are pointing downwards. Elevated and addorsed when the wings are spread upwards and back to back. Addorsed and inverted when the wings are back to back and the tips are pointing downwards.

SOARING: when flying upwards.

VOLANT: when flying horizontally.

THE FALCON: Unless otherwise blazoned the falcon is represented as close. When it has bells thonged to its legs it is blazoned as belled and jessed. The falcon resembles an eagle but it has a smooth head, whereas the head of an eagle is tufted.

THE SWAN: The swan is found in heraldry as a charge, a crest, supporters and a badge. It is shown as close unless specified otherwise.

THE MARTLET: The martlet, an heraldic bird of the swallow family, is represented without legs or feet.

THE PARROT: The parrot is blazoned as a popinjay.

Eagle displayed from a brass, 1410

Eagle displayed filling the shield

Eagle's head couped

Griffin's head erased

Falcon volant

Dove, wings addorsed and inverted

Popinjay, collared

Falcon belled

Dove, dexter wing elevated & inverted

Martlet

Owl, close

Eagle collared, wings addorsed

Swan, ducally gorged & chained wings displayed & inverted

Fig. 44. Charges: Birds

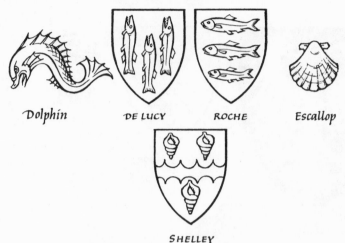

Dolphin      DE LUCY      ROCHE      Escallop

SHELLEY
Fig. 45. Charges: Fish and Shells

## Fish and Shells (Fig. 45)

Fish are found as charges, crests and supporters; they are usually represented true to nature. Different kinds of fish are found as a play on names, e.g. *Azure, three roach naiant* (swimming fesswise)—Roche; and *Gules three luces* (pike) *haurient* (rising palewise to the surface for breathing)—de Lucy.

THE DOLPHIN: has a characteristic form, it is usually bent in a curve and termed embowed. When blazoned proper it is shown as green with scarlet fins and tongue.

SHELLS: The most common shell in heraldry is the escallop, or cockle-shell emblem of St. James, and far less frequently the whelk shell, e.g. *Sable a fess engrailed and three whelk shells or*, for Shelley.

## Natural Objects

### TREES, PLANTS AND FLOWERS (Fig. 46)

Trees are usually blazoned proper and therefore shown in their natural colouring growing out-of the ground. They are termed eradicated if they are uprooted. A fruit tree is fructed. An oak tree may be acorned (Fig. 69).

A tree or plant should display in a conventional form its characteristics. A few typical oak leaves and acorns clearly drawn within the outline of the tree will

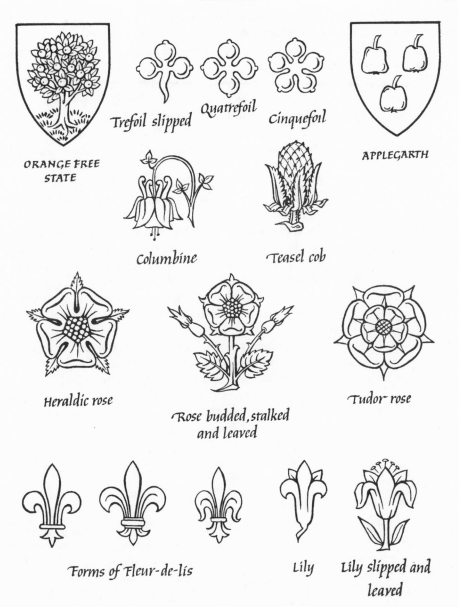

Trefoil slipped  Quatrefoil  Cinquefoil

ORANGE FREE
STATE

APPLEGARTH

Columbine  Teasel cob

Heraldic rose

Rose budded, stalked
and leaved

Tudor rose

Forms of Fleur-de-lis  Lily  Lily slipped and
leaved

Fig. 46. Charges: Trees, plants and flowers

indicate the oakishness of an oak better than a naturalistic oak tree on a small scale, and the same is shown in the arms of the Orange Free State (Fig. 46).

Fruits of all kinds are found as charges, as in the arms of Applegarth—*Argent, three apples slipped gules.*

Flowers may be shown true to nature and some have a stylized heraldic form. When the stem is attached the plant or flower is termed stalked; when the leaves are attached to the stem it may be termed stalked and leaved.

THE TREFOIL is a conventional leaf with three lobes, usually with a short stem when it is termed *slipped.*

THE QUATREFOIL and CINQUEFOIL are conventional forms consisting of as many petals as implied in the name.   They are blazoned as pierced when there is a hole in the centre of the form.

THE ROSE: The stylized form of rose usually has five petals of equal size, with seeds in the centre of the flower and the tips of the sepals appearing between the petals.   The tincture must be blazoned.   The rose may be barbed and seeded proper in which case the sepals will be green and the seeds in the centre gold.   The seeded centre may be designed in a variety of ways.   Only the flower is depicted unless the blazon indicates that it is slipped and leaved.

THE TUDOR ROSE: There are various forms of Tudor rose but it is usually shown as the white rose of York superimposed on the red rose of Lancaster.

THE FLEUR-DE-LIS: The ancient and beautiful fleur-de-lis is a memorable heraldic charge which has varied considerably in style at different periods and in different countries.   It is thought to derive from the form of the iris.

THE LILY: The lily as a charge is distinct from the fleur-de-lis.   It may take a variety of formalized shapes.

## Celestial Charges (Fig. 47)

THE SUN: The sun is represented by a disc, sometimes with a human face; it may be blazoned in his splendour or in his glory when the disc will be surrounded with a variable number of rays alternately straight and wavy.

SUNBURST: Several rays of sun issuing from a cloud.

THE MOON: The moon is usually a crescent with the horns upwards; when shown sideways with the horns to the dexter the moon is waxing, with the horns to the sinister it is waning.

STARS, or ESTOILES: Stars usually have six or eight rays, either wavy or alternately

Sun in splendour                    Sun-burst

Crescent

Estoile or star

Fig. 47. Celestial charges

wavy and straight sided; it must be distinguished from the star shaped charge called a molet (Fig. 52).

CLOUDS: Clouds may be represented as cumuli, as in nature. They are frequently represented in a conventional manner with a nebuly line (Figs. 24*e*, 34 Mercers, Fig. 52*a*).

## Inanimate Objects

### THE CROSS (Fig. 48)

The cross is important as an ordinary and also as a charge. Its value as a religious symbol has led to a proliferation of its plain and decorative forms and to the terms applied to them.

The plain cross may be varied with ornamental border lines (48*a*). It may be voided, having the centre of the cross removed (48*b*), and it may be fimbriated (48*c*), i.e. have a border of a different tincture on the same plane as the cross: *Sable a cross gules fimbriated argent*—City of Durham (48*c*).

The proportions of the cross of St. George (48*d*), *Argent a cross gules*, is considerably narrower in relation to the field than the same cross when charged. The cross in the arms of the City of York (48*e*)—*Argent on a cross gules five lions passant guardant or*, requires width to carry the charges on it. In the arms of the See of Durham (48*f*)—*Azure a cross or between four lions argent*, the cross is narrower between the charges. The proportions are again adjusted in the arms of Cambridge University (48*g*)—*Gules a cross ermine and four lions passant guardant or, with a book gules upon the cross*, as both the cross and the field are charged (Plate 20).

There are numerous crosses where the limbs do not extend to the edge of the shield as they do with the ordinary. These crosses are generally drawn with limbs

*a.*
Cross raguly

*b.*
Voided

*c.*
Fimbriated

*d.* ST. GEORGE

*e.* CITY OF YORK

SEE OF DURHAM

*g.* UNIVERSITY OF CAMBRIDGE

Fig. 48. Charges: The Cross
*g.* Designed by Reynolds Stone. Reproduced by
permission of the Cambridge University Press

of equal length and the ends of the limbs may be squared or treated decoratively.
The width of the cross may be varied.   Crosses are borne singly or in groups.

Some examples of crosses found as charges are shown in Fig. 49 and many other
crosses are variations of these:

*a, b, c.*   The Cross patonce has the ends shaped like paws (pattes)—from this is
derived the cross flory and floretty.

*d.*   The Cross moline and its variants derived its form from the mill-rind or fer-de-
moline.

*e.*   The Crosslet or Cross botonny.

*f.*   Cross crosslet fitchy.   Crosses sometimes have a spiked foot described as fitchy.

*g.*   Cross potent having crutch shaped ends.

*h.*   Cross formy with splayed arms and flat ends, also termed paty.

*i.*   The Tau, or Cross of St. Anthony has no upper limb.       *j.*   Maltese Cross.

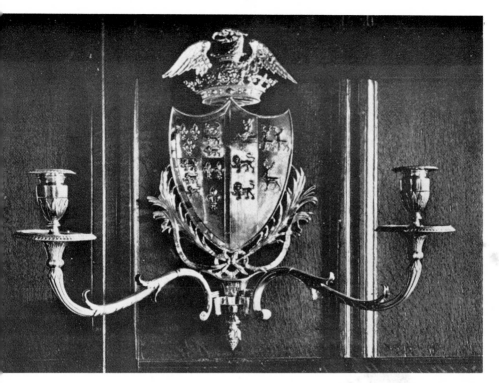

a. Silver sconce, 1702, with the badge and arms of the foundress, the Lady Margaret Beaufort, impaling the arms Thomas Rotherham, Bishop of Lincoln.   St. John's College, Cambridge.   *Crown Copyright*

George I silver snuff box engraved with the arms reke of Carbery. English, about 1720.  *Victoria lbert Museum.   Crown Copyright*

13c. George I silver snuff box engraved with the arms and crest of the Weavers' Company.  English, 1723. *Victoria & Albert Museum.   Crown Copyright*

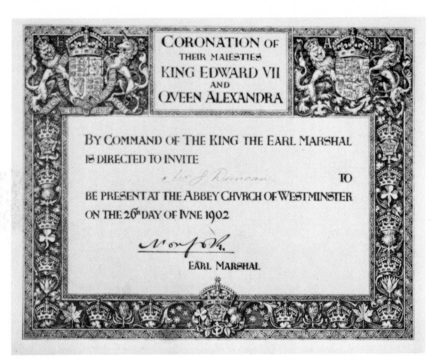

14a. Invitation to the coronation of King Edward VII and Queen Alexandra. Designed by G. W. Eve

14b. Bookplate designed and engraved by George Friend, showing healdic tinctures by hatching

14c. Bookplate designed and engraved by George Friend

he Letters Patent granting alterations to the Armorial Bearings of Edward Harold Cole, Esquire, and confirming
rms of Perry, the Patent also assigning a Device or Badge. In the margin the arms of Cole are depicted together
1 standard bearing the quartered arms of Cole and Perry and the Badge and motto of Cole. The arms of Perry
1e Badge of Cole appear in the text. At the top are the Royal Arms flanked by the arms of the Earl Marshal
gland on the left and the College of Arms on the right. The seals of Garter and Clarenceux Kings of Arms
1ndant below the signatures. The border is illuminated with roses, fleurs-de-lis, acorns and pears. The official
ption was engrossed on vellum by W. T. Lovegrove and illuminated by Gerald Cobb at the College of Arms,
*Reproduced by courtesy of A. Colin Cole, Esq.*

16b. Arms designed for a visitors' book, Holy Trinity Cathedral, Suva, by Sheila Waters; struck by Roger Powell and Peter Waters

16a. Ampleforth Abbey Roll of Benefactors. Manuscript and drawing for the arms' block by Margaret Alexander. Binding in gold and blind tooling by S. M. Cockerell

16c. Arms of Sutton Valence School, Kent, in coloured leather, designed by Sheila Waters for a ceremonial table made by Edward Barnsley

16d. Arms of the Diocese of Conor. Lino-cut display in the Church of Ireland hall, Portstewar Robert G. Sellar

Fig. 49. The Cross. *a* Patonce. *b* Flory. *c* Floretty. *d* Moline. *e* Crosslet or cross botonny. *f* Cross crosslet fitchy. *g* Potent. *h* Paty or Formy. *i* The Tau cross. *j* Maltese cross

Fig. 50. Arms of the City of London and Emblem of the French Republic designed for the *Radio Times* by C. W. Bacon

Fig. 51. Arms of the City of London and the Emblem of Thailand. Designed by L. S. Haywood for the *Radio Times* on the occasion of the State Visit

The objects which appear as charges are so numerous that only those which have a stylized heraldic form, and therefore may present a problem to the designer, are described and illustrated here (Fig. 52).

ANCHOR: Placed palewise, unless otherwise blazoned.    The points are termed flukes.

ARROW: An arrow is said to be armed, or barbed, and feathered or flighted of a tincture.    It is placed palewise unless otherwise blazoned.    The position of the point should be indicated in the blazon.

AXE: Placed erect with head in chief and cutting edge to the dexter unless otherwise blazoned.

BOOK: The blazon should indicate whether the book is open or shut, how it is bound and clasped and any inscription it may bear.

BOUGET, or WATER-BOUGETS: Two skins with a wooden cross-piece between them, used as a vessel for carrying water.    This may take various forms.

BOW: The long-bow is depicted unless the cross-bow is specified.    The blazon should indicate whether the bow is straight or bent and stringed.

BUCKLE: The shape should be indicated in the blazon, also the position of the tongue, whether the point of it is in chief, or fesswise with the point to the dexter or sinister.

CALTRAP: An implement with four conjoined spikes, placed in the ground with one spike upwards, used in war to impede horses.

CASTLE: Usually depicted as two or three round towers with battlemented tops connected by a wall containing an archway and arrow slits.

CATHARINE WHEEL: Usually a wheel with six or eight spokes and as many short curved blades on the rim.    Emblem of St. Catherine.

CHESS ROOK: The rook or castle of chess represented heraldically by two wing-like projections on the base of a chess piece.

CLARION: A wind instrument, possibly a mouth organ with handle; or panpipes represented heraldically in various forms.

CUP: A goblet with stem and foot.    It is termed a covered cup when it has a domed top.

FETTERLOCK: A shackle and padlock which takes various forms and was borne as a badge.

GARB: A sheaf of wheat unless any other grain is specified.

LYMPHAD: An ancient galley with a single mast and sail unless otherwise blazoned. The sails may be furled.

MAUNCHE: A lady's sleeve with pendant lappet, of the time of Henry I.

MILL-RIND or FER-DE-MOLINE: The iron fixed at the centre of a mill-stone.    It can take various shapes.

Anchor  Arrow  Battle-axe  Book  Book open

Bouget  Bow  Buckles  Caltrap  Castle  Catharine wheel

Chess-rook  Clarion  Covered cup  Fetterlock  Garb  Lymphad

Maunche  Mill-rind  Molet or mullet  Molet pierced  Pheon  Tower

Fig. 52. Charges: Inanimate objects

Molet or Mullet: Derived from molette, or spur-rowel, this charge has straight
rays, usually five in number.   It is a molet pierced if it has a hole in the
middle.   It must not be confused with an estoile.

Pheon: A barbed arrow-head, borne point in base unless otherwise specified.

Tower: Consists of a single tower to distinguish it from a castle.   A tower has an
archway in the base and arrow slits; it may have turrets rising from the
battlemented top.

Weapons, tools and other objects now obsolete are recorded in heraldry.   Care
should be taken to discover what is intended before attempting to copy unfamiliar
charges from any source.   For example, in representations of the arms of the Worshipful Company of Curriers the currier's shaving knife is more often than not
depicted with a cross-piece attached to each of the handles.   'This can only be
attributed to a desire for artistic symmetry which has on occasions further corrupted
the handles by giving them trefoil-like endings or forming them into ornamental
crosses.   In fact the true currier's knife, which is used as a form of plane or spoke-
shave to pare the skins after their initial treatment by the tanner or tawer, has a
cross-piece only on one of the two handles.'[1] (Fig. 52a.)

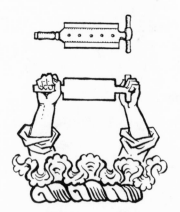

Fig. 52a   *Above:* A currier's shave.
*Below:* Crest of the Worshipful Company of Curriers. *On a wreath or and
azure out of clouds proper two arms
embowed carnation* (flesh-coloured), *the
shirt sleeves folded beneath the elbows
argent, in the hands a shave argent
handled or*

[1] *The Armorial Bearings of the Guilds of London.*   John Bromley.   Warne & Co., 1960.

Fig. 53. From the painting on the Lislebon panel, 14th century, in Winchester Cathedral. Sir William de Lislebon wears coat of mail, surcoat and ailettes. His arms on shield and ailettes are: *per pale sable and argent a chevron counterchanged*. Lady Anastasia his wife wears her husband's arms semy on her mantle

# ARMOUR

Armour and armorials are so closely linked that some knowledge of medieval armour, and an appreciation of its influence on heraldic design, is not only of interest but of value to the designer.    In the Middle Ages every part of a knight's equipment was used for the display of his armorial devices in order to establish identity.

Armorial devices were introduced in the 12th century; they soon became systematized and began to be handed down from father to son.    The shield was painted with the bearer's arms; the charges were embroidered or painted on his surcoat which was worn over mail; they also appeared on the trapper of his horse; the pennon on his lance and on his banner.    About the middle of the 13th century rectangular pieces of leather called ailettes (Fig. 53) came into use as protection to the shoulders and these also were decorated with armorial devices.    Crests were displayed on the helm and on the poll of chargers, and the development of the crested helm also strongly influenced heraldic design (Fig. 55).

The structural lines of the medieval shield, which was often made of cuirbouilli and stiffened with wood, may have been the origin of some of the ordinaries. Shields were curved horizontally in order to deflect a blow and were boldly decorated with armorial devices.    The shield could be hung from the bearer's neck by the thong, or guige, which was attached to it and inside were loops of leather, called enarmes, by which it could be held.

Fig. 54. Figure of a Knight wearing plate armour, ailettes, helm and camail with a lion on his surcoat. Detail from a 14th-century stained glass window, Tewkesbury Abbey, Glos.

Heraldic art reached its greatest height in the 14th century and among the finest examples of work of that period, exhibiting outstanding qualities of heraldic design, are the arms of Edward the Black Prince in Canterbury Cathedral (Fig. 55). The effigy on his tomb shows the prince protected by a suit of plate armour; mail only

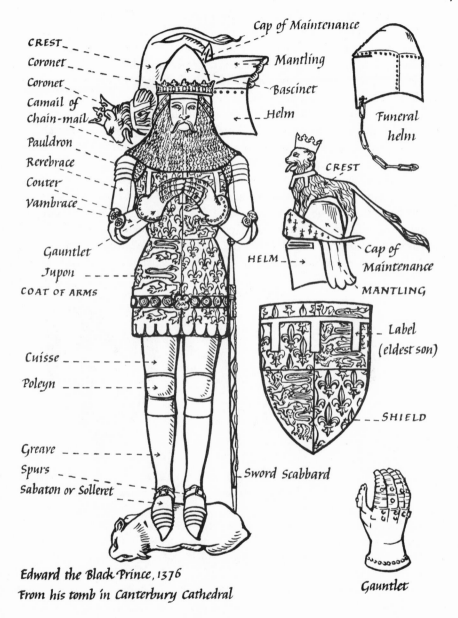

CREST
Coronet
Coronet
Camail of
Chain-mail
Pauldron
Rerebrace
Couter
Vambrace

Gauntlet
Jupon
COAT OF ARMS

Cuisse
Poleyn

Greave
Spurs
Sabaton or Solleret

Cap of Maintenance
Mantling
Bascinet
Helm

Funeral
helm

CREST

HELM

Cap of
Maintenance
MANTLING

Label
(eldest son)

SHIELD

Sword Scabbard

Edward the Black Prince, 1376
From his tomb in Canterbury Cathedral

Gauntlet

Fig. 55. Armour. Edward the Black Prince, 1376. Taken from his tomb in Canterbury
Cathedral

appears at the throat, armpits and the calves of his legs.   On his head is a bascinet, encircled with a coronet; beneath his head lies his great helm, which is surmounted by the crest, the cap of maintenance and the short lambrequin or mantling.   The royal crest shown here is the lion statant, crowned and differenced with a label as the prince was the eldest son of Edward III; the belt and sword are also decorated with lions. The feet are supported on a lion.

The prince is wearing a short surcoat or jupon on which are his arms: France and England quarterly and a label of three points argent.   In the same chapel are preserved the shield, sword, surcoat, helm and gauntlets which were carried at his funeral in 1376; exact replicas of these were made in 1954 and now hang above the tomb.   The vigorously drawn lions of England on the effigy and on the shield itself and the jupon are well arranged and the fleur-de-lis of France are graceful and well proportioned.   The handsome shield has right-angled corners and elegant curving sides.   The tomb is decorated with small enamelled shields of the arms of the prince and also of his shield 'for peace' blazoned *Sable three ostrich feathers argent, slipped through scrolls inscribed 'Ich Dien'* (Fig. 56).   A detailed study of the heraldry

Fig. 56. Shield 'for peace'

in Canterbury Cathedral is an inspiration to a young designer.   Attention should also be paid to the fine collections of armour in the Tower of London and the Wallace Collection.

The drawings of the Black Prince in Fig. 57 were made from a true-to-scale construction kit model eight inches high, one of a series of historical figures produced by Airfix.   The helm, bascinet, visor, shield and crest can all be taken on and off. The author has found it helpful to draw this figure from various angles and watch the play of light on the insignia.   It enhances and is vital to one's grasp of heraldry to see it in the round; these plastic models, and those called 'Swoppets', of medieval knights in armour on horseback and on foot are an attractive form of self-education.

It could be said that if the Middle Ages were the age of chain mail, then the 14th

Fig. 57. Sketches from a model of the Black Prince in which he is wearing a surcoat or jupon over a suit of plate armour. In sketch *a* camail protects the throat. *b* The vizor on the bascinet is raised, seen from the front: the shield on the left arm is suspended from a guige, or strap, over the right shoulder. *c* Side view showing the vizor raised. *d* Vizor closed. *e* Three-quarter view wearing the great helm which is surmounted by the crest, cap of maintenance and short lambrequin. *f* Front view in which the crest, turning with the helm, is now seen facing forward giving it a very different silhouette

century was an age of transition from mail to the predominance of plate armour in the 15th century. Arms and armour are frequently found as charges in heraldry; swords, battle-axes, spears, bows, arrows, gauntlets, spurs, greaves and helms among others, all of which should be drawn to look like the real weapons and protective armour. Whole figures of men in armour, usually plate armour, are found as crests and supporters and occasionally as a charge.

# THE HELMET

The helmet has a vital place in the design of an achievement of arms; in its central position it acts as a link between shield and crest and its size and shape are important factors.

Armorial helmets are frequently depicted too small in scale in relation to the shield, they may be fantastic in shape and bear little relation to real armour; no human being could see out of such helms even if the head could get inside them. With the improvement in heraldic design which has taken place during this century it has now become the practice to depict a practical helm of the style that could have been worn in combat, war or tournament.

The shape of the helm, like that of the shield, has varied with the centuries. In the 13th century the great helm, cylindrical in form, with a flat or pointed top, was worn over chain mail. In the 14th century a close-fitting cap of steel was introduced and to this was attached a protection for the neck made of chain mail called a camail. The great helm was worn over the bascinet in combat, which proved a somewhat clumsy combination and led to the bascinet being strengthened and provided with a visor, and the camail was replaced with a metal gorget.

By the 15th century the great helm was worn only in tourneys and there were three types: the tilting helm which had a slit designed to give vision, when the head was inclined for combat; the helm with a visor, worn open or closed; the helm with an opening in front of the face protected by a grille or bars of metal lattice work.

A few great helms, or tilting helms, have survived in England, owing to the ancient practice of suspending the funeral insignia over the tomb of the deceased. Illustrated in Fig. 58 are the Melbury helm, the Brocas helm and the helm found in the triforium of Westminster Abbey. There are also the Windsor, Haseley, Coleshill and Wallace Collection helms, which are cylindrical and rather more squat in shape. From the artist's point of view a knowledge of these tilting helms is of great value in heraldic design. It is worth a designer's time to make drawings from the actual helms, should opportunity arise.

The designer can judge a fair relationship in size between the helm and the shield by considering whether the wearer of the helm he has depicted could carry a shield of the size he has drawn in the same achievement.

When tournaments ceased in the 16th century the lighter form of helmet was substituted for the great helm. In the reign of James I rules began to dictate the position and type of helmets to be used to denote the rank of the holder of armorial bearings. Unfortunately, as regards position, these rules still obtain today although

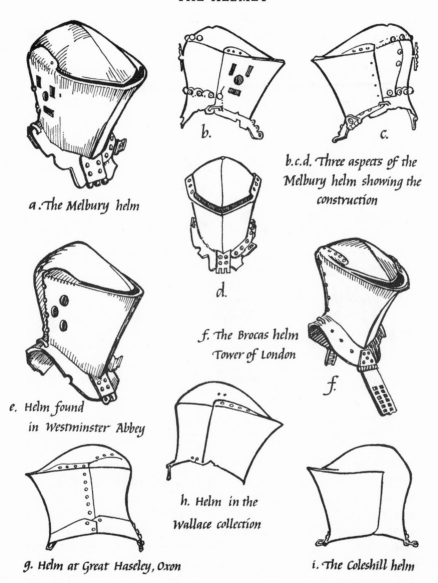

a . The Melbury helm

b.

c.

b.c.d. Three aspects of the
Melbury helm showing the
construction

d.

f. The Brocas helm
Tower of London

f.

e. Helm found
in Westminster Abbey

h. Helm in the
Wallace collection

g. Helm at Great Haseley, Oxon

i. The Coleshill helm

Fig. 58. The Helmet

on the wane (Fig. 59). The Sovereign and princes of the Blood Royal have a helm of gold with five, six or seven gold bars, placed affronty, i.e. full-faced. Peers have a helm of silver showing five gold bars; it is placed sideways, usually to the dexter. Baronets and knights have a vizored helm of steel with the vizor raised and the helm is placed affronty. Esquires and gentlemen have a steel helm, either a closed helm or one with the vizor down; it is placed sideways, usually to the dexter.

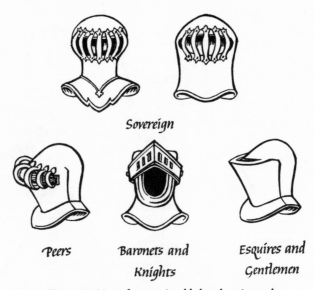

*Sovereign*

*Peers*              *Baronets and*          *Esquires and*
                       *Knights*              *Gentlemen*

Fig. 59. Position of conventional helms denoting rank

Silver and steel helmets may be garnished with gold. Open helmets may show the crimson or blue lining of silk which covers the padded lining within.

These conventional helmets certainly assist in the easy recognition of rank. The front facing helm is a problem in design; not only is it an unattractive object with the vizor raised, but the crest on top is normally drawn from the side position and in some cases has even been so modelled. Often the crest itself has been so ill chosen that it would be impossible to identify the owner from it unless it was placed in profile and the resulting anomaly of the crest astride the helm instead of facing the same way is one of the saddest features of present-day heraldry.

When the owner has two crests the helms may both face to the dexter, or face one another, in which case the dexter crest must turn with the helm. If the result of making two crests face each other is that they seem to be fighting each other, as

Fig. 60. *Earl of Buckinghamshire* (Dom Anselm)
Arms: Quarterly 1st and 4th arg. a saltire gu.,
between four eagles displayed az. Hampden.
2nd and 3rd sa. an estoile or between two
flaunches ermine. Hobart
Crests: 1. A talbot ermine collared and lined
or terminating in a knot gu. Hampden. 2. A
bull passant per pale sa. and gu. bezanty a ring
in its nose or. Hobart

Fig. 61. *Earl of Warwick* (J. Forbes Nixon) Arms:
Sa. on a cross five pellets, a bordure engrailed or.
Crests: 1. Out of a ducal coronet gu. a demi-swan
wings elevated arg. beaked of the first. 2. A bear
arg. muzzled gu. supporting a ragged staff arg.
Supporters: Two swans', wings inverted arg.
ducally gorged gu.

might happen with, say, crests of a demi-dragon holding an arrow and a lion
ramping with a sword, it is better to make both face to the dexter, avoiding if
possible the appearance that one is stabbing the other in the back (Figs. 60, 61).

As gentlemen's, knights' and peers' helms would still be recognizable whatever
their position, there can be no merit in regarding this as fixed and it is recommended
that if the nature of the crest demands it the helm should always be shown 'moving'
in the same direction as the crest. It is no detraction from this suggestion that
Royal Helms might then be confused with peers' helms (for both would find
themselves placed in the same position) because the Royal Helms are always
identifiable by the Royal Crown and Royal Crest of the royally crowned lion
that surmounts them (Fig. 107).

When there are more than two crests all should be placed on helms which rest
on the shield; the practice of putting the other crests 'in the air' on either side is to
be deplored.

It is not desirable to include a helm in an achievement unless there is a crest for it
bear.

Fig. 62. Torse or crest wreath

## THE TORSE or CREST WREATH

The torse or crest wreath was a silken favour which encircled the top of the helm over the mantling It may have been inspired by the Arab head-dress seen by the Crusaders.   It is now represented as a twist of two or more colours, which appear in six alternate folds of soft material.   Unless otherwise blazoned the folds of the torse, like the mantling, are of the colours, i.e. the main metal and colour in the shield of arms.   The first fold on the left of the wreath is the metal and the last is the colour, although of course in a wreath that has two metals, e.g. argent, gules and or, the last mentioned metal would be on the right (Figs. 62a, b).

Despite the still prevailing formula in patents of arms that express the crest to be granted as 'upon a wreath', the wreath looks its best when it gives the impression of being wreathed about the crown of the helm; it may take on a curve when seen in perspective from below, and it will usually hide the join of the crest to the helm, but at times the top of the mantled helm may be allowed to show.

As already mentioned, the phrase usually found in the blazon relating to the crest placing it, 'On a wreath of the colours...', may account for the unfortunate manner of depicting the crest wreath as a rigid bar with the crest perched upon it and both precariously balanced on top of the helm; this is both bad in design and false in construction and it is to be hoped that there will be official reversion to the 15th-century formula in patents, when the crest was stated to be on the *helm*, and the wreath described separately from the crest and in relation to the mantling, a truer affinity.

The crest should appear to be fixed to the helm and the wreath to encircle the brow of the helm at the base of the crest.   There are times when variations of design are expedient and the limbs of animals may be made to straddle the crest wreath.

The custom of representing the crest on a crest wreath when it is used without the helm and mantling, has led to the torse being depicted as a rigid bar (Fig. 62c). It is usually more successful when designed as if the wreath is slightly curved, as shown in Fig. 62b.

Fig. 63. CRESTS. *a* Tilting helm and crest of Sir John Gostwick, 1541. Worthington Church, Bedfordshire. *b* Funeral helm, a Soldan's head of carved wood, crest of George Brooke, Lord Cobham, 1558. Cobham Church, Kent. *c* Close helm, 1530. Wooden crest, two arms embowed, in the hands a sheaf of arrows, added for the funeral of Sir Edward Barkham, 1634

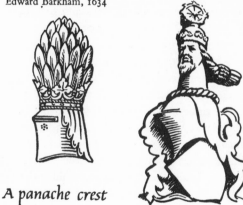

*A panache crest*

*d*                    *e*

*e* Detail from the tomb of Lewis Robsart, Lord Bourchier, K.G., 1431. Westminster Abbey

# THE CREST

Heraldic crests came into use early in the 14th century. They were splendid objects made of a fairly lightweight material, such as moulded leather, thin wood, or canvas stretched over a wicker frame. They were gilded and painted in bright colours and firmly fixed to the top of the helm (Fig. 63*a*, *b*, *c*). The helm and crest of the Black Prince, preserved at Canterbury, weighs 7 lb. 2 oz. (Fig. 55).

An early crest often consisted of a plume of feathers, called a panache, (Fig. 63*d* shows the panache crest from the seal of Edmund Mortimer, 1372), but there was an increasing popularity for crests representing birds, beasts, human beings and monsters. Half a creature or a head alone was more convenient than a whole and could be made larger and more easily recognizable. The animal faced the same way as the wearer of the helm and this must always be borne in mind when designing today. Flat objects, such as the sun, were fixed edgeways on to the helm or in such a way that they were recognizable from an angle (Fig. 63e), and objects that did not lend themselves to such treatment were not chosen as crests, another principle that has been forgotten in recent centuries.

The tournament was a spectacular form of sport. The courage of the combatants, their powerful horses, magnificent armour and all the colour of heraldry combined to enhance the prestige of the antagonists and the great nobles and their ladies who watched and applauded. Consequently heraldic design was a matter of interest to all. One can imagine the severe criticisms that would have been meted out to an artisan who failed to make a well poised crest for his master's jousting helm. The design of many types of crests remained sensible and lively until tournaments became obsolete in the 16th century, when crests and helms were no more seen in use and heraldic blazons became increasingly complex and pictorial.

Today all the skill and ingenuity of the designer is required to fit on to a helm some of the crests which were conceived on paper and could never have been made in the round, e.g. *Upon waves of the sea, the stern of a Spanish man of war, all proper, thereon inscribed San Joseff* (with motto over: Faith and Works) for Nelson.

A crest was intended to face the same way as the helm, so that when the helm turned the crest turned with it. The designer's task today would be simplified if the nature of the crest determined the way the helm should face in heraldic design. The rule typical of 'paper heraldry' at its worst, that the helm in the armorial bearings of the Sovereign, knights and baronets should be placed affronty and the helm in the armorial bearings of peers and esquires should be in profile is sanctified by three hundred and fifty years observance, and it often poses a problem for the designer. In Fig. 105 it is impossible to make a demi-griffin rampant face the same way as a helm affronty, and a lion couchant guardant supporting a banner is little better, but at least the creature in this case is facing the same way as the helm. A griffin's head between two wings expanded arg. on a helm affronty is more convincing as the body is affronty even though the head is facing to the dexter.

The problem of designing the crest to fit the helm is less difficult with the combination of a crest affronty and an esquire's helm in profile; by a nice adjustment, and some manipulation with helm and crest, both can face the same way without breaking the rules.

However the only satisfactory way out of this impasse, created by failure to accept that the crest was something worn on a helm which itself was worn, is the

COUNTY BOROUGH OF HALIFAX

AT A SPECIAL MEETING OF THE
COUNCIL OF THE
COUNTY BOROUGH OF HALIFAX
holden in the Council Chamber at the Town Hall
on Wednesday the Twenty-Sixth day of May, 1954
The Worshipful the Mayor ( Councillor Harold Pickles J.P.)
in the Chair.

It was resolved unanimously :-

THAT in pursuance of Section 259 of the Local
Government Act, 1933, the Council do admit

THE RIGHT HONOURABLE
THE LORD MACKINTOSH
OF HALIFAX,
D.L., LL.D., J.P.
to be an
HONORARY FREEMAN OF THE
COUNTY BOROUGH OF HALIFAX
in recognition of his eminent services to the nation
and borough.

The Right Honourable
THE LORD MACKINTOSH
OF HALIFAX, D.L., LL.D., J.P.
attended and in pursuance
of the resolution above set
out the Honorary Freedom
of the Borough was duly
conferred upon him and the Roll of Honorary
Freemen was subscribed by him on Tuesday the
Twenty-Ninth day of June, 1954.

The Common Seal of
the Mayor, Aldermen
and Burgesses of the
County Borough of
Halifax was hereunto
affixed in the presence of -

Mayor

Town Clerk.

17a. Conferment of the Honorary Freedom of the
County Borough of Halifax on the Right Honourable
the Lord Mackintosh of Halifax, D.L., LL.D., J.P.
Vellum scroll by Thomas W. Swindlehurst, lettering in
scarlet, blue and black, with name in gold. At the
top the arms of the County Borough of Halifax, the
arms of Lord Mackintosh of Halifax beneath, painted
in colour and gold

17b. Blue leather case blocked in gold

18b. The Dragon of Henry VII, the White H of Hanover and the Lion of England, Gardens

18a. The Yale of the Beauforts. *Ministry of Public Building and Works*

18c. The Griffin of Edward III and the I Bull of Clarence, Kew Gardens

Queen's Beasts, designed by James Woodford, R.A.

19b. Arms of the Midland Bank, Clapham, in Portland stone. James Woodford, R.A.

9a. The Royal Arms designed by James Woodford, R.A., or use on Government buildings at home and abroad. *Ministry of Public Building and Works*

9c. Arms of H.R.H. Princess Elizabeth with supporters and the rose, thistle, shamrock and leek emblems. Designed by James Woodford, R.A., for Cheltenham College. *Courtesy Cheltenham Newspaper Company Ltd.*

ALEXANDER
HENRY LOUIS
2ND BARON
HARDINGE
of PENSHURST
PC·GCB·GCVO·MC
BORN
17TH MAY 1894
DIED
29TH MAY 1960

20a. Top to an altar tomb in Portland stone designed Kindersley. Fordcombe Churchyard

20b. Arms of Cambridge University in Clipsham Key signed by David Kindersley. Botanic Gardens, Cambrid

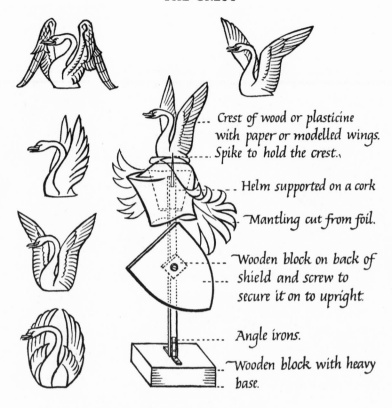

Crest of wood or plasticine
with paper or modelled wings.
Spike to hold the crest.

Helm supported on a cork

Mantling cut from foil.

Wooden block on back of
shield and screw to
secure it on to upright.

Angle irons.

Wooden block with heavy
base.

## Scale model of shield, helm and crest

Fig. 64. Scale model of shield, helm and crest showing the swan crest turned through
various degrees and with the wings varying in style and arrangement

abandonment of the position rules of the helm, and there are increasing signs that
English practice is at last moving in this direction (Scottish practice having long
done so), it being well over fifty years since Fox-Davies condemned the then
modern abortions: 'The crests of the present day are the crying grievance of modern
English heraldry. . . . We shall not obtain a real reform, or attain to any appreciable
improvement, until the "position" rule as to "helmets" is abolished. . . .'

It can be a help even when making a two-dimensional design to model the crest
boldly on a small scale in Plasticine and fix it to the top of a model helm or a sub-
stitute round object (Fig. 64); this method is especially helpful when designing

GHD

winged creatures as it is difficult to make a pair of elevated wings look convincing in the drawing of a crest.

A simple scale model of shield, helm and crest is shown in Fig. 64. The helm is hollow and rests on a cork fixed to an upright. A spike in the helm holds the crest in position. The wooden shield has a block on the back and is secured to the upright by a screw which enables the shield to be tilted at any desired angle. The crest is made separately of wood or Plasticine. The complete model can be placed at a suitable eye-level and observed from differing angles. The eye level chosen should be consistent in the drawing for all parts of the achievement. The position of crest and helm can be nicely adjusted. The mantling is made in cooking foil, or paper pressed round the helm and the edge suitably scalloped.

An article, 'Heraldry in the Round' by John Ferguson, A.R.C.A., 'Coat of Arms', Oct. 1962, illustrates a set of little models constructed in wood and paper and painted in gouache, an admirable idea.

Crests should appear fixed to the helm and not merely perched upon it. In the 18th and 19th centuries crests and helms were drawn too small in scale, as were the niggardly charges on the shields in the heraldic stationer's engravings of the time.

The scale relationship between crest and helm is one of common sense. The shield, crest and helm may each be similar in size, or the helm and crest together may equal the area of the shield.

A crest is intended to be borne upon a helm in association with a crest wreath, chapeau or crest coronet. The chapeau is now limited to crests granted to peers; but in their case it is usually tinctured gules lined with ermine. The crest is placed on top of the cap, or a creature may straddle the cap with its feet on the brim. The cap is rested on the helm with the mantling flowing from under it (Fig. 55).

Crest - coronet

Fig. 65

Right: Fig. 66a

Badge of the
BRITISH RAILWAYS BOARD

Fig. 66. British Railways Board. Alternative style: the objects are set round the rim of the coronet without finials

The crest coronet is often misleadingly termed a ducal coronet (Fig. 65). It bears no relationship to ducal rank and must not be confused with the styles of coronets worn by peers and peeresses according to their degree. There are several other forms of crest crown as well as the well-known mural, naval and eastern crowns, and from all these, crests which issue therefrom are granted. As a matter of design, coronets, which have their finials springing naturally from an engrailed rim, look much better than when objects such as roses and acorns are set directly round the rim (Fig. 66).

A crest cannot exist without a coat of arms, but it has become an unfortunate practice to represent the crest standing upon the crest wreath, apart from a helm, and both floating unsupported above the shield. If the crest has perforce to be shown without helm or mantling then it must stand upon a crest wreath, and the wreath should still appear as if composed of two pieces of material twisted together, and not inadvertently resemble an iron bar or a French loaf (Fig. 62c).

# THE MANTLING or LAMBREQUIN

From early times a small mantle or piece of material was shown attached to the helm and hanging down over the shoulder of the wearer. It probably originated as a protection against the heat of the sun on the metal. The decorative possibilities of the mantling were fully exploited by medieval craftsmen and it is in the treatment of this feature that the designers' skill has full scope. The mantling can be severely simple or employed as an elaborately ornamental space-filling device.

In early representations mantling barely extended beyond the base of the helm (Fig. 67a, b, c), the edges were sometimes scalloped, in keeping with contemporary costume and a large tassel might be attached to the end. The mantling hung down at the back of the helm only and retained its cloak shape for some time. It was then shown divided into two longer and narrower pieces which appeared on either

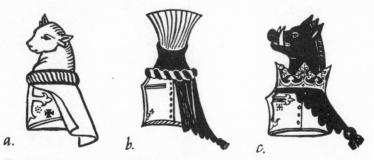

a.          b.          c.

Fig. 67 a Helm, crest, wreath and mantling from the Hastings brass at Elsing, 1347.
d Helm with crest, torse and mantling from the Harsick brass at Southacre, 1384.
c Helm, crest, coronet and simple form of mantling from the stall-plate of Ralph, Lord Bassett, 1390

side of the helm.   Both the edges became deeply serrated, the larger leaf-like serrations being further sub-divided; some early mantlings were represented entirely of feathers, usually accompanying a feathered crest (Plate 3, Fig. 68).   The principal divisions of the mantling were then made to extend throughout the whole length of the cloth and they became increasingly elaborate and ornamental (Fig. 69b), sometimes resembling complicated strap-work, scroll work, or seaweed, the resulting

Stall-plate of Richard Beauchamp
Earl of Warwick, 1423

Fig. 68. Mantling or lambrequin

a.  Crest and mantling of the
GIRDLERS' COMPANY

b.  MILNE-WATSON

Fig. 69a, b Mantling or lambrequin.   Styles of
mantling

design being far removed from the original material attached to the helm of a jousting knight.

The material of mantling should appear to be a fairly heavy cloth which, though firmly fixed to the helm by the crest wreath, is made to flow out in graceful controlled twists and flourishes. The weight and pattern of the mantling can help to balance a crest but it should not interfere with the clear outline or distract the attention from the crest itself.

In the graphic design of a full achievement the mantling may be so short that it does not reach as far as the supporters. It may also be designed to flow down generously beside or behind them and the shield they are holding. It should not be allowed to give a confused effect, the supporters should remain clear and the mantling subordinate. The purpose of the design will usually dictate the quantity of mantling suitable to it. For elaborate arrangements a study of acanthus decoration from classical sources and carved Renaissance heraldry will prove helpful.

A sculptor in designing an achievement must obviously visualize the mantling in relief, and a designer working on the flat will make a more coherent design if he too considers his mantling three dimensionally, so that the twists and serrated edges appear to be formed from one piece of cloth, and are not a patchwork of unrelated pieces of colour and metal.

In pursuit of this three-dimensional understanding the author has found it helpful to make a mock model (Fig. 64). A piece of kitchen foil cut in the shape of a cape or semicircle is fixed on to the top of a model helm three inches high (a round object such as an orange will do instead) and the foil is then cut into three wedge-shaped sections. Viewing this mock-up on eye level, with the helm in profile, one piece of the foil is brought forward of the far cheek of the helm and all three of the pieces are twisted and turned; their edges are cut into serrations. By this means both the play of light and shade and the balance of the inside and outside shapes of the mantling, which in the design will be in different tinctures, can be assessed.

The balance of mantling in a black-and-white drawing is not so difficult to solve. The problems arise in arranging the flourishes of coloured cloth with the metal lining, particularly on either side of an esquire's helm which, facing to the dexter, tends to show too much of the coloured outside at the back of the helm on the sinister, and too much of the metal lining in front of the helm on the dexter.

The practice in early blazons was varied, the principal metal and colour in the arms being distinct from the mantling and crest wreath. In the 15th century particoloured mantlings were frequent and today mantlings, e.g. azure and gules, with either one or two metals tincturing the lining, are re-appearing. As a vehicle for the badge, the mantling has not been permitted to resume its role, although one outstanding modern example is found in the Achievement of the Heraldry Society

A trick of the arms of the HERALDRY SOCIETY

BADGE OR DEVICE

Fig. 69c A trick of the arms of the Heraldry Society showing the badge borne
on the mantling

(Fig. 69c).  In grants of the 16th and 17th centuries the mantling is almost always
gules doubled argent, whatever the tinctures of the torse.   Mantling of that period
was often represented as ending in gold tassels.   If this attractive conceit is used today
the tassels should be tinctured gold.   The present practice is for mantling to be 'of

the colours', that is the main colour in the arms is lined (or doubled) with the principal metal.

Some recent Grants of Arms specify in the blazon the tinctures of the mantling. If these are not mentioned it is prudent to find out the tinctures of the torse and mantling.

Formerly an ermine lining was allowed not only to peers of the realm, but also to commoners, now it is the exclusive right of royalty. Care must be taken that the ermine tails follow naturally the curves towards the base of the cloth; this extends to other charges or devices which may powder the mantling, for example, the crest and mantling of the Worshipful Company of Girdlers (Fig. 69a): *In a cloud, with the sun issuing therefrom the figure of St. Lawrence, vested azure, and holding in his dexter hand a gridiron and in his sinister hand a book or.* Mantling: *Azure doubled ermine powdered with suns issuing from clouds.* It is surprisingly easy to draw charges or devices upside down on the twists of the mantling. A crest wreath may also be of ermine and a colour and the tails should run naturally with the twists. (See p. 94, 'Torse' and Fig. 62d.)

Fig. 70. A simplified version of the arms of the British Medical Association, designed by William Gardner for general publicity purposes. The design will reduce to less than the 1¼" diameter required for a letterhead

# THE SUPPORTERS

Supporters, according to some writers, originated when seal engravers required to fill the empty space between the shield and margin of a circular seal (Fig. 2). For this purpose badges in the form of creatures were a common choice and a 'beast badge' in later heraldry seems to have taken on the role of a supporter for the arms. The duty of the various human, bird or beast forms which have been or are granted as supporters is, as their title implies, to guard and support the shield of arms.

Human beings usually face the spectator (Fig 70) and hold the shield between them by one hand only, the other sometimes supporting the helm or crest; the actual attitude of supporters is not always specified in blazon, and animal supporters usually assume an upright or rampant position facing one another on either side of the shield; if the head is turned this should be specified in the blazon, but heads of human beings can be turned so best to suit the whole design.

All supporters should be designed in a vigorous manner within the space allowed by the composition; upholding the shield with their limbs—not leaning or sprawling over it in a lazy way as if unequal to the task. The legs of birds and animals should not be twisted into unnatural and visually uncomfortable positions. The conventional arrangement of supporters may be disregarded, unless the blazon is compelling, by designers of some experience when armorial bearings have to be planned to fill an unusual space. Although not often observed in present-day official practice, supporters when they have collars which are charged should be depicted with the charge running round the whole of the collar as if the latter were chased or ornamented throughout with these lesser devices. When an escutcheon or other object is pendant from a supporter's collar it should be shown hanging down in a natural way and not as if stamped on one shoulder like a cattle-brand (Plate 21a, c).

The right to a grant of supporters is now generally limited to peers and peeresses of the realm, Knights of the Garter, the Thistle and St. Patrick, Knights Grand Cross and Knights Grand Commanders of other orders. Supporters are granted to some corporate bodies. Spiritual peers do not use supporters.

Supporters are granted by Letters Patent and care must be taken not to confuse authentic supporters with such forms as angels and amorini which were frequently designed to uphold a shield or crest for purely decorative or religious reasons. There is a charming anomaly in having the pride of lineage in this world supported on sumptuous tombs by carved images of angelic beings of the next. The cherubs on the panel at the foot of Henry VII's tomb in Westminster Abbey, designed by the Italian Torregiani, are a case in point.

# THE MOTTO

The motto was sometimes derived from a war-cry, but it was usually a brief phrase expressing a loyal, pious or moral sentiment, or a play on the name of the bearer. In England the motto is not usually included in the grant of arms by letters patent, so no authority is required for the use of one. It may be in any language, Latin and Old French are common. Even Braille has been aptly used, on Lord Fraser's motto scroll.

The custom is for the motto to be written, painted or incised on a scroll or ribbon which flourishes beneath the shield. It is not compulsory to use a scroll, but should it be used all the words of the motto must be on the same side of the scroll and the design of the folds and curls should be practical and solid.

Motto scrolls are sometimes designed so that they appear to be breaking into several pieces because the perspective of the folds and loops has not been grasped. The scroll should either be even in width throughout its length, or taper intentionally and not merely because of poor drawing. In designing motto scrolls the author has found it a help to cut a long strip of fairly thick paper about one inch wide, holding it at different levels, to roll and turn it until it shapes to the design, at the same time studying the play of light and shade on the curves and along the thickness of the upper edge. The folds should be made to suit the number of words and the style and colour of lettering should be in keeping with the achievement in period and purpose. The ends of the scroll may be curled up or cut into fish-tails and flourished. The back of the scroll may be a different colour from the front.

The decorative value of the scroll is enhanced by the fact that it frequently forms the base line of the design of the whole achievement and should therefore help to give stability and balance.

## THE COMPARTMENT

Supporters are designed to hold up the shield and in order to do so they need an adequate support for their paws, feet or claws. They are sometimes designed as if balancing precariously on the motto scroll by a big toe or one desperate claw. This does not make a seemly support for men in armour or rampant elephants nor can it give a visual sense of stability to the creatures or to the design. At one period the ornamental scroll work popularly known as the gasbracket was a favoured support and architectural pediments have also been used, and are often most suitable.

Another solution is to design a mound, or compartment as it is termed, at the base of the design on which to stand the supporters and rest the shield. The mound may take the form of a grassy hillock on which badges or floral emblems can be displayed, or it can appear as stony ground or a ploughed field where these are appropriate. For the support of sea-creatures undulating waves stylistically treated are both apt and decorative.

# PART TWO

In Part One the components of an Achievement of Arms have been analysed and described.   Although this book cannot aim to cover the whole field of systematic heraldry there are certain additions and variations to armorial bearings which are of particular interest to craftsmen engaged in interpreting blazons into designs.   Some of these are described here.

## DIFFERENCING and CADENCY

The primary purpose of armorial bearings is that they should be distinctive not only of their owner but of individual members of his family as well; they should distinguish younger branches of the family from that of the head, since all persons legitimately descended in the male line from a common armigerous ancestor may bear his arms.

For this purpose a method of differencing arms for cadency was evolved at the time when arms still served for the purpose of recognition in tournaments and on seals, by which the original arms were slightly modified, by adding a border or altering a tincture for instance, while retaining their principal features.   An alternative method of differencing introduced at an early date was by the addition of a minor charge, called a cadency mark (Fig. 71), which did not alter the armorial bearings in any way and could be removed or varied according to individual changes in the family.   In the 15th century these marks became standardized, with a definite cadency mark to denote each son in order of seniority and since about 1500 this has remained the system.

The following charges are those borne for cadency by sons on their paternal arms; these marks remain constant with the exception of the label for the eldest son which is removed on the death of his father.

## Cadency Marks

| | | |
|---|---|---|
| a. Eldest son | a label | |
| b. Second son | a crescent | |
| c. Third son | a molet | |
| d. Fourth son | a martlet | |
| e. Fifth son | an annulet | |
| f. Sixth son | a fleur-de-lis | |
| g. Seventh son | a rose | |
| h. Eighth son | a cross moline | |
| i. Ninth son | a double quatrefoil | |

Fig. 71. *Marks of difference for cadency*

A mark of cadency is usually borne in the chief of the shield, except in a quartered coat when it is placed in the centre, where all the four quarters meet; unless it belongs to one coat only in which case it is placed in that quarter only.

The label is a narrow stripe which extends from side to side of the shield, and the three pieces pendant from it should be adjusted to suit the design. The label is frequently drawn unduly wide with short, ugly wedge-shaped pieces hanging from it.

Royal cadency is marked exclusively by a label consisting of a stripe, argent, with four or five pieces hanging from it; the label itself is differenced with small charges.

# AUGMENTATIONS

An honourable addition to armorial bearings is called an augmentation. From the 14th century onwards these augmentations of honour have been granted to commemorate historic events or outstanding exploits.

An augmentation may take the form of an additional charge, or a coat of arms borne as a quartering or inescutcheon, or an additional crest.

The augmentation to his arms granted to Thomas Howard, Earl of Surrey in 1513 commemorated his victory over the Scots at Flodden Field (Fig. 31*b*); to his arms: *Gules, a bend between six cross-crosslets fitchy argent*, there was added an escutcheon of the Royal Arms of Scotland with the lion cut in half and pierced through the mouth with an arrow, this being placed on the bend (Figs. 72*e, g*). The Duke of Norfolk and members of the Howard family include the augmentation in their arms to this day.

At the time of the Restoration the first Sir Winston Churchill was among those who received augmentations to their arms, as will be seen in Fig. 105, and his descendant, the late Sir Winston Churchill, bore this augmentation in the first and fourth quarters of his arms, together with the augmentation granted to his ancestor the first Duke of Marlborough to commemorate his victories; this is borne as an escutcheon displayed over all in the centre chief point of the shield.

The Duke of Wellington was granted in 1814 an augmentation to his arms (Fig. 87): *Quarterly 1 and 4 Gules, a cross argent between in each quarter five plates, Wellesley, 2 and 3 Or, a lion rampant gules, Colley.* The augmentation, consisting of the Union Badge of the United Kingdom, is displayed over all in the centre chief point.

# MARSHALLING

The original intention of a coat of arms was the practical one of personal identification. Marshalling is primarily the combination of two or more coats of arms on one shield to indicate the alliance of families by marriage or by descent. It is also employed to indicate the holding of office.

There are three ways of marshalling arms:

IMPALEMENT: In this method the shield is divided in half palewise (Fig. 72*a*) with a central vertical line and in each of the two halves an entire coat of arms is shown, e.g. *Argent on a bend azure, three cinquefoils pierced or*, for Cookesey impaling *Gules,*

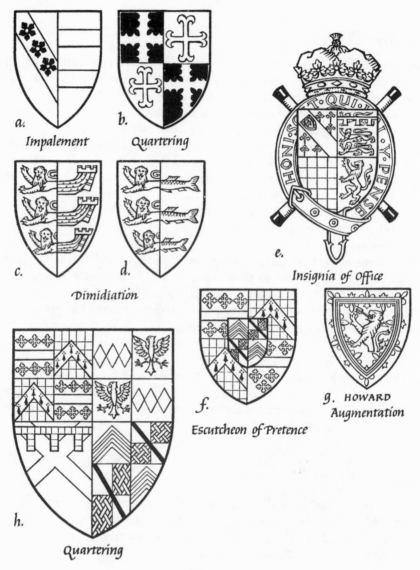

Fig. 72.

*a* Cookesey impaling Harcourt. *b* William, Lord Willoughby. *c* Cinque Ports. *d* Great Yarmouth. *e* Duke of Norfolk, Earl Marshal of England. *f* Richard Beauchamp, 5th Earl of Warwick; on an escutcheon of pretence the arms of Clare and Despencer. *g* Augmentation granted to Thomas Howard, Earl of Surrey, for Flodden, 1513. *h* Arms of Richard Nevill, Earl of Warwick and of Salisbury, the 'Kingmaker'.

*two bars or*, for Harcourt. This method of displaying the arms of husband and wife may be seen on seals and is still in use today.

Impalement is also used as a temporary means of marshalling to combine the arms of an office with those of the holder, e.g. an archbishop or bishop with those of his see (Fig. 96); a dean with those of his cathedral; a King of Arms with the arms of his office; the head of a college or a regius professor with those of his college or faculty respectively. It should be noted that the arms of the office appear on the dexter side of the shield, the arms of the holder on the sinister.

Official insignia may also be shown with armorial bearings: for example, the Duke of Norfolk, Earl Marshal of England, places two gold batons tipped with black saltirewise behind his shield (Fig. 72e). Quarterly I. *Gules, a bend between six cross-crosslets fitchy argent; on the bend an escutcheon or, charged with a demi-lion rampant, pierced through the mouth by an arrow, within a double tressure fleury-counter-fleury gules*, for Howard. (Figs. 31b, 72g.) II. *Gules three lions passant guardant in pale or, in chief a label of three points argent*, for Thomas of Brotherton. III. *Chequey or and azure*, for Warren. IV. *Gules a lion rampant or*, for Fitzalan. The arms are encircled with the Garter and surmounted by a ducal coronet.

Marshalled arms require special consideration when insignia, which are appropriate to one partner in a marriage and not to the other, have to be included in an achievement. The head of a college or a mayor, for example, may place two shields side by side, the shield on the dexter bearing the official arms impaled with his own and the shield on the sinister bearing his personal arms with those of his wife or impaled with his own in pretence. An escutcheon of pretence (Fig. 72f) is a shield bearing a distinct coat of arms charged upon the centre of another shield larger in size, e.g. the arms of Richard Beauchamp, 5th Earl of Warwick, and on an Escutcheon of Pretence the arms of Isabella, heiress of Thomas Despencer, Earl of Gloucester. Husband and wife each had a quartered shield before marriage.

Knights of the Garter, and knights, commanders and companions of other orders, who are entitled to their respective insignia may display two shields, one bearing their paternal arms round which are placed the insignia of the order, and the other bearing their own arms with those of their wife either in pretence or impaled. In order to balance the design of this 'married' shield with the other, a garland or wreath, which has no heraldic significance, may be placed round the second shield (Fig. 73).

DIMIDIATION: In this method the two coats of arms to be marshalled are halved palewise by a central vertical line, the dexter half of one and the sinister half of the other appearing joined on the respective halves of the shield. This method was

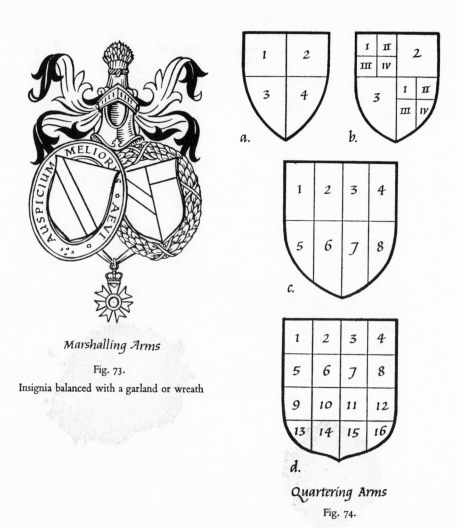

Marshalling Arms

Fig. 73.

Insignia balanced with a garland or wreath

Quartering Arms

Fig. 74.

abandoned as it led to quaint and misleading results.  Two examples of dimidiated arms still in use are: *Gules, three lions passant guardant or, dimidiating, Azure, three ship's hulls fesswise in pale argent*, for the Cinque Ports (Fig. 72c); and *Gules, three lions passant guardant or, dimidiating Azure, three herrings naiant argent*, for Great Yarmouth (Fig. 72d).  In the former the bodies of the lions appear conjoined to the sterns of the ships and in the latter to fish-tails.

21a. Arms of the British Broadcasting Corporation in slate, designed by David Kindersley

Arms of Homerton College in Ketton stone, Cam-
e, designed by David Kindersley

21c. Arms of Viscount Nuffield at Nuffield
College, Oxford, designed by David Kindersley

22a. British Medical Association seal. Note how the twists of the mantling and the flames from the torches in the crest are designed by William Gardner to lead the eye round to the band of lettering. *By courtesy of the B.M.A.*

22b. H.M. Queen Elizabeth II. English shilling. Desig and modelled for die-making by William Gardner, 1952. T three lions passant guardant are well accommodated in shield, the semicircular base of which carries the eye round the echoing curve of the Tudor-like crown above. *From Royal Mint Annual Report, 1952. By permission of the Contro of H.M. Stationery Office.*

22c. Privy Council Seal. A lively rendering of the lion and unicorn supporters dancing over the floral emblems of the United Kingdom which are surmounted by the St. Edward crown. Designed by William Gardner

22d. Plaster model for H.M. Royal Signet or Minister State seal, designed by William Gardner. The field of shield, the Garter and the background behind the band lettering are all on one plane which makes the most of v low relief. At this stage the modelling on the charges freely rendered.

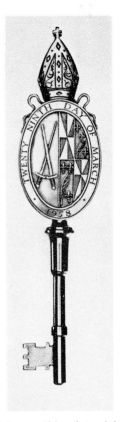

23*a*. Church Wardens' staves, St. Peter's Church, Nottingham. Designed by Leslie Durbin, M.V.O.

23*b*. Ceremonial key designed for the Pastoral Aid Society by Leslie Durbin

23*c*. Silver casket given by the Bank of England to the Clearing House Bankers. Designed by Leslie Durbin

24b. Badge of Office for the De[puty] Mayor of Bury St. Edmunds, desi[gned] and made by Francis J. C. Cooper

24a. Heraldic detail of the mace presented to the Worshipful Company of Farmers by the late Lord Courthorpe. The bull is in red enamel with gold stars. Designed by Francis J. C. Cooper

24c. Masters's jewel for the Worshipful Company of Scientific Inst[rument] Makers, designed and made by Francis J. C. Cooper, in gold n[ounted] with sapphires, diamonds and onyx. The arms represent an optical [...] the crest is Minerva's head, the supporters: Faraday, in a red gown, [holding] his coil, for the electrical instrument makers, and, Newton, in a [...] gown, holding his telescope, for the optical instrument makers

QUARTERING: Quartering (Fig. 72b) is the marshalling of two or more coats of arms on one shield by dividing the shield into four and placing a coat of arms into each division, for example the arms of Lord Willoughby from his stall-plate. If two coats only are to be quartered the more important is placed in 1 and 4, the other in 2 and 3 (Fig. 72b). With three or more coats the principal coat, which is usually the paternal, is placed in the first quarter and repeated in the fourth, the others being in the second and third quarters in order of importance (Fig. 72f). A quarter may itself be quartered in order to contain more coats, when it is said to be quarterly quartered, e.g. Fig. 72h. The arms of Richard Nevill, Earl of Warwick and of Salisbury, the 'Kingmaker', combined with those of his wife. At a time when heraldry had ceased to have a practical use in warfare complicated arms such as those reflected the concentration of power and possessions and symbolized ties of kinship and family pride.

When the number of coats to be displayed demand many quarterings the shield may be divided by vertical and horizontal lines into 8, 16 or 24 sections, still called quarters (Fig. 74). If there is an uneven number of coats to be shown the arms in the first quarter may be repeated in the last quarter.

The practice of marshalling arms, reaching its height in Tudor times, when pride of family and the showier aspects of heraldry had taken the place of its practical use in war and tournament, is described by Sir Anthony Wagner in 'Historic Heraldry of Britain' as follows:

'A husband impales his wife's Arms with his own, unless she be her father's heir or coheir in blood (that is to say, if she has no brothers), when he displays them on an escutcheon of pretence, superimposed in the centre of his own shield. In the latter case only, the children acquire a right to quarter the Arms of their mother's family (and any quarterings previously acquired in the same way by that family) with their father's. [Fig. 72f.] In this way a shield of many quarterings indicates a succession of heiress marriages, so that the bearer represents in blood all the families whose Arms he quarters.'

A man does not require to display all the quarterings to which he is entitled. A widower ceases to impale the arms of his late wife, but the impaled arms may be placed on a memorial or hatchment.

## BEARING OF ARMS BY WOMEN

It has become the custom for the arms of widows and unmarried women to be displayed upon a lozenge (instead of upon a shield) without crest or accessories. The lozenge (Plates 14b, 19c) is often an inconvenient shape for the display of arms and may lead to the distortion of the charges, and a roundel, or a lozenge with its bounds expanded in a suitable way, are preferable as a shape.

A Lozenge bearing the arms of a spinster (Fig. 75) may have a knot of ribbon at the top; this is merely decorative and has no heraldic significance.  Unmarried daughters bear their paternal arms and any mark of cadency included in these arms, but they add no mark of cadency to denote their own position in the family.  An unmarried woman holding office such as a mayor or head of a college may, while she holds office, impale the arms of the corporation or college with her own on a lozenge, with the official arms on the dexter side.

*Lozenge bearing the arms of an unmarried lady*

Fig. 75. Bearing of Arms by Women

A married woman bears her paternal arms marshalled with those of her husband, by impalement or escutcheon of pretence.  A married woman holding office will impale the arms of a corporation or college on a shield on the dexter side, and on the sinister side the arms of her husband with her own impaled or in pretence.

A widow continues to bear the combined arms of her late husband and herself, but places them on a lozenge without helm or crest.

# CROWNS and CORONETS

## THE ROYAL CROWN

The Great Seals and certain coins of the realm show some of the changes that have taken place in the form and enrichment of the Royal Crown of Great Britain through the centuries.

The conventional representation of the crown (Fig. 76) used in a flat design of the Royal Arms consists of a circlet jewelled, thereon four crosses paty (one and two halves are visible) and four fleurs-de-lis (two heads are visible). Of the four arches quartering the circlet, three are visible, enriched with pearls; these arches curve upwards, flatten out slightly at the top and meet at a depression in the centre; at the juncture rests an orb banded with jewels, surmounted by a cross. The cap within the circlet is of crimson with the ermine lining showing below the rim. The crown in current use in official designs of the Royal Arms is discussed on page 166.

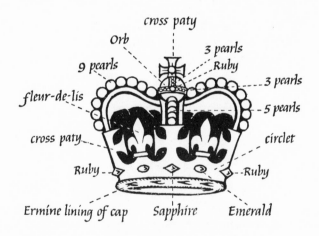

*The St. Edward Crown*

Fig. 76.

## ROYAL CORONETS (Fig. 77)

The coronet of the Prince of Wales is similar to the Royal Crown but with one arch spanning the circlet instead of two. The younger children and brothers and sisters of the Sovereign have similar coronets but without an arch. The circlet is chased as if jewelled but is not set with gems.

Grandchildren of the Sovereign who are issue of sons in the direct line show a coronet with two crosses paty, four fleurs-de-lis and two strawberry leaves, of which one cross, two fleur-de-lis heads and two strawberry leaves are visible in a drawing.

Children of the Sovereign's younger sons, and sons of the Sovereign's brothers, have four crosses paty and four strawberry leaves. Children of the Sovereign's daughters with the style of Highness have four fleurs-de-lis and four strawberry leaves. In every case the cap, if shown, is crimson lined with ermine, with a gold tassel on the top.

REPRESENTATIONS OF THE CORONETS OF PEERS (Fig. 77)

*Duke:* A circlet of silver gilt, chased as if jewelled but not set with gems, heightened with eight conventional strawberry leaves of which three and two half-leaves are visible. The coronet of a duke must not be mistaken for a ducal coronet which is used in place of a crest wreath or as a charge (Fig. 65).

*Marquess:* A circlet as above heightened with four gold strawberry leaves alternating with four silver balls, termed pearls, and slightly raised on points. One whole leaf, two half-leaves and two silver balls are visible in a drawing.

*Earl:* A circlet as above with eight high points, five visible, each topped with a silver ball, and between each point a strawberry leaf.

*Viscount:* A circlet as above set with sixteen silver balls, touching one another; nine are visible.

*Baron:* A plain silver gilt circlet set with six large silver balls of which four are visible.

Coronets are usually worn with a crimson cap lined with ermine and surmounted with a gold tassel. An achievement of arms may show the coronet with or without the cap, resting on the shield with the helm, crest and mantling placed upon or (if without the cap) within it. It is not essential that the coronet should be shown in this position, but better results artistically are thereby achieved (Plate 20a).

The coronet without cap is often shown surrounding the helm, or as much larger in diameter, but although in fact the coronet should fit the head more closely it helps to balance the design for the size to be somewhat exaggerated. It is a mistake of fact to represent the ermine lining of the cap below the rim of the coronet and omit to draw the cap itself inside the coronet (Fig. 103).

Sovereign's children (except the Heir Apparent) and brothers and sisters.

 Duke.

 Marquess

 Earl

 Viscount

Baron

Above: Fig. 77. Crowns and coronets

On left: Fig. 78. Arms of Queen's College, Dundee. Designed by William Gardner in black and white on an ornamental italianate shield for a letterhead. Also used as a book stamp in gold on cream leather. Note the interlacing of crosses and fleurs-de-lis in the crown

 King - of - Arms

 Mural crown

 Naval crown

 Astral crown

 Eastern crown

 Celestial crown

Fig. 79.
Crowns

FURTHER CROWNS AND CORONETS (Fig 79)

*King of Arms:* The crown of a King of Arms is silver gilt, it has sixteen acanthus leaves alternating in height, set erect on a circlet which bears the inscriptions: Miserere mei Deus secundum magnam misericordiam tuam. Nine leaves and the first three words are visible.

Crowns may sometimes appear as charges in coats of arms and where no type is specified a crest coronet or crown of fleurs-de-lis may be shown.

Those most often met with are:

*Mural Crown:* The mural crown is represented as masoned and embattled. It may be of any tincture. It is common in civic heraldry.

*Naval Crown:* A naval crown consists of a circlet on which are mounted alternately the sterns and sails of ships.

*Astral Crown:* Consists of a circlet on which are mounted four stars, three visible, each between a pair of elevated wings.

*Eastern Crown:* Consists of a circlet which has eight points, five of which are visible.

*Celestial Crown:* Similar to an eastern crown with each point surmounted by a star.

# ORDERS OF KNIGHTHOOD and INSIGNIA OF HONOUR

*Baronets.* The hereditary Order of Baronets is a degree below the Peerage. Baronets bear as an augmentation on their shields an escutcheon argent charged with a sinister hand erect, couped at the wrist and appaumy gules (Fig. 80a). The escutcheon is usually placed in the dexter chief or centre chief of the shield. The red hand is the badge of Ulster; it was adopted as the mark of a baronet when the order was founded in 1611 by James I at the time of the colonization of Ulster.

Baronets wear an oval badge on ceremonial occasions containing a shield argent with a sinister hand gules ensigned with the imperial crown, within a border decorated with roses for baronets of England, shamrock for baronets of Ireland, roses and thistles for baronets of Great Britain, roses, thistles and shamrock for baronets of the United Kingdom.

The holder of a baronetcy is entitled to suspend the badge, on its orange ribbon with a dark blue edge, below the shield.

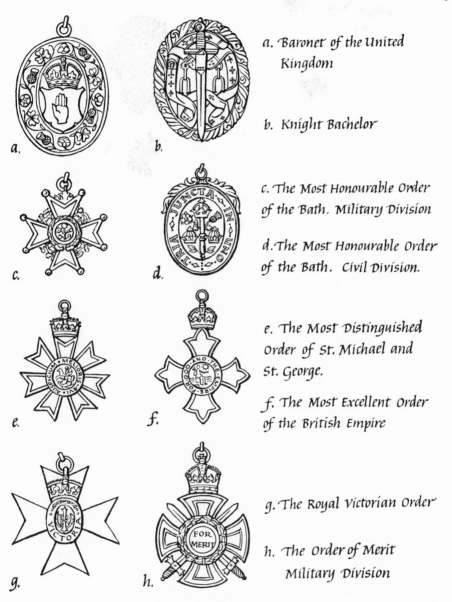

a. Baronet of the United Kingdom

b. Knight Bachelor

c. The Most Honourable Order of the Bath. Military Division

d. The Most Honourable Order of the Bath. Civil Division.

e. The Most Distinguished Order of St. Michael and St. George.

f. The Most Excellent Order of the British Empire

g. The Royal Victorian Order

h. The Order of Merit Military Division

Fig. 80. Orders of Knighthood and Insignia of Honour

ORDERS OF KNIGHTHOOD

Today there are two main classes of knighthood: knights of one of the Orders of Chivalry and Knights Bachelor.

*Knights Bachelor.* Knights Bachelor represent the ancient knighthood which existed before the Orders of Chivalry were founded. The badge of a Knight Bachelor is an oval medallion of vermilion enclosed by a scroll and thereon a cross-hilted sword, belted and sheathed, pommel upwards, between two spurs, rowels upwards, the whole set about with the sword-belt, all gilt (Fig. 80*b*). The badge may be placed below the shield.

*The Most Noble Order of the Garter* was founded in 1348 by Edward III. The insignia which is most likely to concern a designer of heraldry is the blue Garter with gold edge and buckle, bearing in gold letters the inscription: 'Honi soit qui mal y pense' (Shame be to him who thinks shame of it). The Sovereign and knights of the order encircle their shields with the Garter and they may also place outside it the collar of the order and its pendant 'George', though few do so. The 'George' is a badge representing St. George on horseback slaying the dragon; it is enamelled in colour. The ribbon is the blue ribbon of the Garter. The collar of gold consists of twenty-four red roses also enamelled in colour, each within a blue garter with the motto in gold, linked by gold knots. All twenty-four roses need not be shown in a design of an achievement (Figs. 105, 107).

Knights of the Orders of Chivalry founded in later centuries followed the custom of Knights of the Garter in surrounding their shields with the circlet bearing the motto of their order. All the Orders of Chivalry have a circlet of a distinctive colour, bearing the motto of the order, but without the buckle or tongue of the Garter. The circlet is edged with gold and the motto is in gold letters.

CIRCLETS AND MOTTOES

The most Ancient and Most Noble Order of the Thistle:
Colour: Green. 'Nemo me impune lacessit' (No one touches me with impunity).
The Most Illustrious Order of St. Patrick:
Colour: Sky blue. 'Quis separabit MDCCLXXXIII' (Who shall separate? 1783).
The most Honourable Order of the Bath:
Colour: Red. 'Tria juncta in uno' (Three joined in one)

*The Most Distinguished Order of St. Michael and St. George:*
Colour: Blue. 'Auspicium melioris aevi' (Token of a better age).
*The Royal Victorian Order:*
Colour: Blue. 'Victoria'.
*The Most Excellent Order of the British Empire:*
Colour: Scarlet. 'For God and Empire'.

The Orders of Chivalry also have their own collar, badge and ribbon. The Knights of the Thistle and St. Patrick may surround their shields with the collar of their order in addition to the circlet. The collar of the Thistle consists of sprigs of thistle alternating with sprigs of rue, from which hangs the badge bearing the figure of St. Andrew.

The collar of the Order of St. Patrick consists alternately of harps and red and white roses; the badge contains a red saltire surmounted by a shamrock charged with three crowns.

Knights Grand Cross of the other Orders of Chivalry may place the collar round their arms. Other knights may use the circlet with the badge of the order suspended from it.

It is not usual to place round a shield the insignia of more than one order; those of the principal order to which a person belongs being preferred. However, if several insignia are to be shown in one achievement, then one circlet only, that of the senior order, is used. If there is more than one collar, that of the senior order is displayed next to the circlet with the insignia of the lesser order on the outside. The badge of the senior order is centred below the shield, with badges of other orders arranged on either side according to their seniority.

Companions of the Bath and of St. Michael and St. George and Commanders of the Royal Victorian Order of the British Empire may surround their shields with the circlet of their order and suspend its badge below (Figs 80*c, d, e, f*).

Members of the Victorian Order and Officers and Members of the Order of the British Empire hang the badge only of the order below their shields (Fig. 80*g*).

Members or Companions of the Order of Merit, the Order of Companions of Honour, and the Distinguished Service Order may hang the badge below their shield; this also applies to the Victoria Cross and other decorations awarded by the Sovereign.

An account of the Orders of Knighthood and Chivalry with a description and illustrations of their insignia, will be found in 'Burke's Peerage and Baronetage' and in 'Debrett'. A designer who is in any doubt about the style or arrangement of insignia in an achievement of arms should seek advice from the College of Arms.

Fig. 81*j* Badge of A. Colin Cole, Esquire.   A Bull's head
erased gules gorged with a Collar ermine flory counter
flory or, attached thereto a line the strands alternately
argent and gold reflexed over the neck and stapled also gold

## THE BADGE

The terms 'badge' and 'crest' are frequently confused.   A crest is the personal
device of its owner; it is borne on a helm and is part of his achievement of arms.   A
badge on the other hand is a distinctive emblem borne separately from shield and
crest as a mark of allegiance, ownership or dependence, and today often to indicate
membership of an armigerous body.   Although sometimes the same device was
used as a badge and a crest, and in composition might derive from a charge in a
shield of arms or from an element of the crest, a badge is not necessarily associated
with a shield or helm.

The badge was originally a simple device boldly drawn and easy to recognize.
It is well to remember that it lends itself more to two-dimensional representation,
particularly if inanimate.   The household badges of the great lords in feudal times
were displayed on standards and on the liveries of their retainers and private armies;
the use of them reached its height in the 14th and 15th centuries.   Plantagenet
and Tudor badges abound on seals, on monuments and as items in architectural
decoration (Plates 6, 7).   Famous examples (Fig. 81) are the planta genista of the
Plantagenets, the bear and ragged staff of the Earls of Warwick, the knots of the
Stafford family, the feathers of the Black Prince, the red rose of the Lancastrians, the
white rose of York, the Tudor rose and the Beaufort portcullis.   An allusive device
was called a rebus, e.g. the boar (verre) of John Vere, Earl of Oxford, the marguerites
of Margaret Beaufort, a hart lying in water for Walter Lyhart, Bishop of Norwich.

The emblems that are still part of the Royal insignia (Fig. 82), the Rose of England, the Thistle of Scotland, the Shamrock of Ireland, are worn by the Yeoman of
the Guard as badges; the Royal Cipher worn by the State Trumpeters and by Her
Majesty's Forces in a badge-like way is considered as an off-shoot of the ancient
practice among her forebears of using crowned-initials as personal devices.   From
the numerous Royal Beasts, inherited by Queen Elizabeth II from the badges of her
forebears, ten were chosen for display at her coronation (Plate 18).   These were
modelled by James Woodford, R.A. and stood guard outside Westminster Abbey.
They were: the Lion of England, the Griffin of Edward III, the Falcon of the

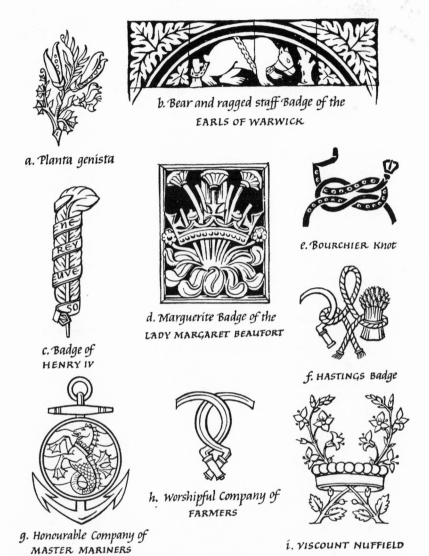

b. *Bear and ragged staff Badge of the*
EARLS OF WARWICK

a. *Planta genista*

c. *Badge of*
HENRY IV

d. *Marguerite Badge of the*
LADY MARGARET BEAUFORT

e. *Bourchier Knot*

f. HASTINGS *Badge*

g. *Honourable Company of*
MASTER MARINERS

h. *Worshipful Company of*
FARMERS

i. VISCOUNT NUFFIELD

Fig. 81. HISTORICAL BADGES: *a* Planta genista, the broom-plant badge of the Plantagenets. *b* Bear and ragged staff badge of the Earls of Warwick, from tiles in Tewkesbury Abbey. *c* Badge of Henry IV entwined with a scroll inscribed with the word Souvereyne. *d* Marguerite badge of the Lady Margaret Beaufort, Westminster Abbey. *e* Bourchier knot from the brass of Sir Humphrey Bourchier, Westminster Abbey. *f* Hastings badge: union of two houses, the knot of Edward Lord Hastings unites the Hungerford sickle with the Peverel garb. TWENTIETH-CENTURY BADGES: *g* Badge of the Honourable Company of Master Mariners. *h* Badge of the Worshipful Company of Farmers. *i* Badge of Viscount Nuffield

Ireland

Ireland

The United Kingdom of
Great Britain & Northern Ireland

The United Kingdom

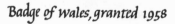

Badge of Wales, granted 1958

The Heir Apparent

Fig. 82. The Badge

Plantagenets, the Black Bull of Clarence, the White Lion of Mortimer, the Yale of the Beauforts, the White Greyhound of Richmond, the Red Dragon of Wales, the Unicorn of Scotland, the White Horse of Hanover; each beast held a shield charged with the appropriate arms or badge.

Personal badges may be granted to armigerous persons and to corporate bodies today; they form part of the heraldic insignia of their bearer, they can be used alone or on a standard and displayed with an achievement of arms or as decorative devices on any background. These personal badges should be differentiated from the impersonal devices used by the Services of the Crown and by colleges, schools and societies.

The badges used by the Services may be thought of as the modern version of medieval badges, serving much the same purpose of ready recognition of personnel and Government property. Some of the divisional unit 'signs' devised in the Second World War were vividly heraldic in character. For information regarding army badges designers should consult 'Heraldry in War: Formation Badges, 1939–45', by Lt.-Col. H. N. Cole.

Badges are also assigned to ships of the Royal Navy. These consist of a roundel on which is displayed a device, usually with reference to the name of the ship, surrounded by a gold border in imitation of a ship's cable and ensigned with the naval crown. At the College of Arms Somerset Herald is Adviser to the Admiralty on Ships' Badges. Information about these badges and permission to reproduce them (they are Crown copyright), can be obtained from the Admiral Superintendent, H.M. Dockyard, Chatham.

In the Royal Air Force badges are used by squadrons, commands, stations and the like; they are also granted to units of the Canadian, Australian and New Zealand Air Forces. The post of Inspector of Royal Air Force Badges is held by Clarenceux King of Arms at the College of Arms. The badge consists of a distinctive device of the unit within a circular frame, the frame varies in design and includes the title of the unit, the motto appears on a scroll below the frame and the badge is ensigned with the Royal Crown.

Fig. 83. White Hart, collared and chained, Badge of Richard II, from a boss in Canterbury Cathedral

# BANNERS

In the 13th and 14th centuries three principal types of flags were emblazoned with heraldic devices, the pennon, the banner and the standard.

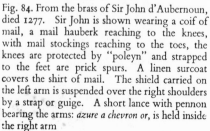

Fig. 84. From the brass of Sir John d'Aubernoun, died 1277. Sir John is shown wearing a coif of mail, a mail hauberk reaching to the knees, with mail stockings reaching to the toes, the knees are protected by "poleyn" and strapped to the feet are prick spurs. A linen surcoat covers the shirt of mail. The shield carried on the left arm is suspended over the right shoulders by a strap or guige. A short lance with pennon bearing the arms: *azure a chevron or*, is held inside the right arm

Fig. 85. From the brass of Sir Simon de Felbrigg, in Felbrigg Church, Norfolk, 1416. Sir Simon in plate armour wears the Garter below the left knee, his shoulders are protected by roundels bearing the cross of St. George, patron of England and the Order of the Garter. He carries the banner of Richard II: *France (ancient) and England* quarterly; impaled by the arms assigned to Edward the Confessor; *Azure a cross patonce between five martlets or*

THE PENNON. The pennon was a small triangular streamer ending in a point or a swallow tail. It was borne below the lance head and was charged with the badge or arms of the bearer (Figs. 84, 87*a*).

THE BANNER. The banner (Fig. 85) was charged with the arms of the bearer and with no other device. It was either square or oblong, the depth being greater than the width. It is an admirable shape for the display of arms and has remained popular on that account. Banners were used at sea as well as on land, and in the Middle Ages even the sails of ships were emblazoned with armorial devices on occasion.

In the 15th and 16th centuries heraldic beasts in stone and metal were employed to support banners on their long staves. Treated ornamentally they were set up on gables and pinnacles as finials and weather vanes (Fig. 86). Banner-bearing creatures also appear on seals and in manuscripts at that period. The banners upheld by lions and eagles on the monument of Lewis, Lord Bourchier, in Westminster Abbey are rather less than a square and a half in area, a good proportion for displaying quartered arms.

When one supporter only is represented as holding the staff on which the banner is flying, it implies that both supporters are alike. When the supporters differ they are shown facing one another and holding the staff between them, with the banner placed centrally above them. The arms must be placed on each side of the banner so that a lion or similar charge faces the staff from which the banner is flying and therefore moves in the direction of its bearer and not the reverse (Fig. 87*a*, *b*, *c*).

Today colleges and municipal corporations possess banners and any armigerous person or corporate body may use one (Fig. 89). Quarterings and marks of cadency are displayed with the arms as on a shield, but crests, badges and other accessories are not included.

Fig. 86. Quartered banner, upheld by an eagle on the monument in Westminster Abbey of Lewis, Lord Bourchier, standard bearer of Agincourt, who died in 1431

a.

b.

c.

Fig. 87 *a* Sir Arthur Richard Wellesley, K.G., P.C., *Duke of Wellington. 1814*
ARMS: Quarterly, 1st & 4th, gu. a cross arg., in each quarter five plates saltirewise, Wellesley. 3rd & 4th, or, a lion rampant gu. ducally gorged or, Colley, and for augmentation in chief an escutcheon charged with the Union badge of Great Britain and Ireland, viz. the crosses of St. George, St. Andrew and St. Patrick conjoined
CREST: Out of a ducal coronet or, a demi-lion gu. holding a pennant gu. one third per pale from the staff arg. charged with the cross of St. George
SUPPORTERS: Two lions gu. each gorged with an Eastern crown and chained or

*b* Francis Wemyss Charteris-Douglas, Earl of Wemyss
ARMS: Quarterly 1st & 4th. arg. a fess az. within the royal tressure gu. Charteris. 2nd & 3rd. or a lion rampant gules, Wemyss
SUPPORTERS: Two swans proper

*c Sir John Poyntz Spencer. Earl Spencer and Viscount Althorp. 1765*
ARMS: Quarterly 1 & 4. Quarterly arg. & gu., on the 2nd & 3rd quarters a fret or, over all on a bend sa. three escallops arg. 2 & 3. Barry of eight or & gu.
CREST: Out of a ducal coronet or a griffin's head arg. gorged with a collar gemelle gu. between two wings expanded and elevated arg.
SUPPORTERS: Dexter a griffin per fess ermine and erminois gorged with a collar flory counter-flory sa. thereon three escallops arg. and chained of the last
Sinister a wyvern ermine gorged and chained as the dexter
Engravings by J. Forbes Nixon in 'Foster's Peerage, 1880'

25b. Gold and enamelled Badge of Office for the Mayor of Brighton, designed by Eric Clements

wel of Office in gold, rubies, pearls and diamonds for the of Bolton, Lancashire, designed by Eric G. Clements

25c. Master's jewel for the Butchers' Company of York. Designed by Leslie Durbin, M.V.O.

26a. Royal Arms painted on wood by L. C. Evetts, affixed to the gallery of the Church of St. Mark, Darlington, 1958. *Photographic Dept., King's College, Newcastle-upon-Tyne*

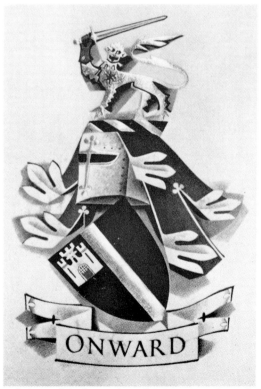

26b. Arms of Castle Ward Rural District Council, Northumberland: *Sable a pale or, in canton a castle argent*. Mantling sable and or. Granted 1963. Designed by L. C. Evetts. *Photographic Dept., King's College, Newcastle-upon-Tyne*

Inn sign. Cadogan Arms, King's Road, London.
ıey, Combe, Reid & Co. Ltd.

27b. Inn sign. Richmond Arms. Designed by Violet Rutter for Whitbread & Co.

ınn sign. Arms of Lord Morpeth: George William rick Howard, K.G., P.C., 1802–1864. Designed olet Rutter for Whitbread & Co.

27d. Hatchment, Sidestrand Church, Cromer, Norfolk. The arms of Viscount Templewood, P.C., G.C.S.I., G.B.E., C.M.G. (dexter Hoare, sinister Lyon), painted in oils and gilded on oak board 3 ft. 2 in. square, by Anthony Wood

28a. Arms of Martins Bank

28b. Marine and General Mutual Life Assurance Society

28d. Arms of Legal and General Assurance Ltd.

28c. Bank of London and South America Ltd.

28e. The Chartered Bank

*The Honourable Company of* MASTER MARINERS

Fig. 88. THE ARMORIAL BEARINGS: Argent on waves of the sea a representation of the ship 'Golden Hind' in full sail all proper, on a chief arched azure a terrestrial globe also proper between two mullets of the field
CREST: On a wreath of the colours in front of a sun in splendour proper a quadrant or
MANTLING: Azure doubled argent
SUPPORTERS: On either side a seahorse proper gorged with a naval crown or, that on the dexter supporting a staff proper headed or flying therefrom the Union flag, and that on the sinister supporting a like staff flying therefrom the Red ensign also proper

THE STANDARD. The standard (Fig. 89) was popular in Tudor times for use in pageants and ceremonial occasions. In shape it was a long narrow tapering flag ending in a rounded point or a swallow tail. It was used for the display of crests, badges and motto. The field and edges were sometimes of the livery colours, i.e. the principal colour and metal in the arms, retainers being dressed in the same colours.

Standards may be displayed by persons and corporations possessing a badge as well as arms. On a standard the arms are shown on the hoist, i.e. next to the staff. The badge which may be alternated with the crest is shown on the fly (which may be of more than one tincture) and may also be crossed diagonally by the motto (Plate 15).

The Royal Banner, now misnamed the Royal Standard (Fig. 90), is the personal banner of the Sovereign. It may be flown only when the Sovereign is present in person. For instance it is flown from the masthead of a ship when the Sovereign is

IHD

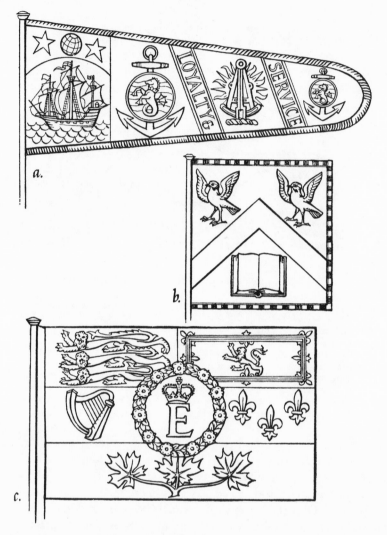

Fig. 89a Standard of the Honourable Company of Master Mariners. The four panels of the Company's standard bear: 1. next the staff, the arms (Fig. 88); 2. the badge; 3. the quadrant of the crest, and 4. in the fly, the badge (Fig. 81)

89b Banner of Sir Ernest Gowers, Knight Grand Cross of the Most Honourable Order of the Bath

89c Personal flag which Her Majesty the Queen adopted for use when in Canada. The arms of Canada are charged in the centre with the Queen's initial 'E' and above it the Royal Crown all within a chaplet of roses, gold on a blue field

on board, and from a car and aeroplane in which the Sovereign is travelling. The Royal Standard is flown from Westminster Abbey when the Sovereign is in the neighbourhood of the Abbey or is attending Divine Service. The Royal Arms which look well on a banner have to be distorted to fit a shape which is a rectangle twice as wide as it is high.

Members of the Royal Family have banners bearing their arms.

Fig. 90. Royal Standard and the flag of the French Republic designed for the *Radio Times* by L. S. Haywood, on the occasion of the State visit of the President

## THE UNION JACK

The Union Flag or 'Union Jack' is the national flag of the United Kingdom. It dates from the Union of Great Britain in 1801 and combines the cross of St. George for England (a red cross on a white ground), the saltire of St. Andrew of Scotland (white cross on a blue ground), and the saltire for St. Patrick of Ireland (red on a white ground) (Figs. 82, 88).

In representations of the Union Jack the broad white diagonal must appear uppermost in the top corner of the flag, i.e. in the half of the flag next to the flagpole. The flag of St. Andrew is above that of St. Patrick in this half but below it in the fly. The flag is frequently displayed upside down. Sometimes it is made incorrectly and it is a difficult banner to draw. Whatever the shape of the flag—square or oblong—if two straight lines cannot be drawn diagonally from corner to corner, thus dividing the Scottish and Irish crosses equally, the flag has not been correctly constructed.

# ECCLESIASTICAL HERALDRY

The armorial bearings of the sees in the Provinces of Canterbury and York are frequently religious in character. They show ecclesiastical insignia such as the pallium or pall of an archbishop in the arms of the See of Canterbury, the croziers and mitres of bishops in the arms of the Sees of Norwich, Chester and Llandaff, the crossed keys of St. Peter in the arms of the See of York, the eagle of St. John the Evangelist in the arms of Liverpool and the sword of St. Paul in the arms of the Sees of Winchester and Exeter (Figs. 91, 92).

See of Canterbury      See of Norwich      See of Durham

Fig. 91. Arms of the See of Canterbury: Azure, an archiepiscopal staff in pale argent ensigned with a cross paty or, surmounted of a pall argent edged and fringed or, charged with four crosses formy fitchy sable

Arms of the See of Norwich: Azure, three mitres labelled or
Engravings by Nixon, 'Foster's Peerage', 1880

Arms of the See of Durham, Azure, a cross or, between four lions rampant argent. (The mitre over the arms is encircled with a ducal coronet)

Fig. 92. Arms of the Archbishopric of York: Gules, two keys in saltire addorsed argent, in chief a crown or. Designed for the *Radio Times* by H. Ellis Tomlinson

Paving tile, Tewkesbury Abbey with the arms of Robert Fitz Hamon, the founder, impaled with the singular cross of the Abbey.

Fig. 93.

Fig. 94. Bishop Wulstan. Clerestory window, Priory Church, Great Malvern 1460–70

Archbishops and diocesan bishops may impale with the arms of their see on the dexter their personal arms on the sinister of a shield. All bishops may ensign their shields with their mitre; they do not use crests, supporters or a motto in association with their arms. Archbishops use a staff headed with a cross. Bishops may place two croziers, in saltire behind the shield. The pastoral staff or crozier of a bishop has a head carved in imitation of a shepherd's crook; originally very simple in formation it later became elaborately carved. In the Eastern Church the pastoral staff of a bishop or abbot terminates in a Tau or crutch.

The mitre is a cap cleft in two parts rising from a circlet. Originally it was made of white linen orphreyed with embroidery, later of damask and cloth of gold, it became richly adorned with precious stones. The style of the mitre has varied considerably at different periods, the early examples being low, and concave at the sides, the later lofty and convex. The simple early shape is preferable to the bulbous type seen in representations in the 17th and 18th centuries. Mitres are tinctured gold and may be jewelled or chased as jewelled, and they are lined with crimson or other rich material (Fig. 94). All mitres have two ribbons called infulae pendent from the rear edge. The error of showing them coming from the inside of the mitre should be avoided. The heraldic. mitre is often drawn too high in proportion to its width, but the dramatic possibilities of both mitres and crowns can be used in design to advantage.

The mitre of the Bishop of Durham rises from a ducal coronet, a token of the former jurisdiction of the bishop as Prince Palatine. The Bishop of Durham may also place a sword and pastoral staff in saltire behind his shield.

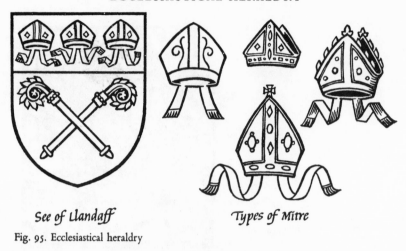

*See of Llandaff*                    *Types of Mitre*

Fig. 95. Ecclesiastical heraldry

Fig. 96. Arms of the See of Canterbury impaled with the arms of Archbishop Laud, the shield surmounted by a mitre. *Roof boss in the choir of Winchester Cathedral.* The dedication of Winchester Cathedral to St. Peter and St. Paul is symbolized in the keys and sword; the arms of the See of Winchester are: *Gules, two keys addorsed* (back to back), *in bend, the uppermost argent, the other or* (joined at the bows, or rings, at the ends) *a sword interposed between them, in bend sinister, the blade silver, pommel and hilt gold.* It will be seen that the manner in which the charges are arranged has varied at different times: on the left are the arms from a carving on the nave vaulting in the Cathedral, on the right the arms boldly carved on a roof boss on the vaulting underneath the tower

In the Victoria and Albert Museum there are fine early examples of mitres and croziers to be seen.

On religious festivals and ceremonial occasions, a banner or flag may be flown from the towers of cathedrals and parish churches. These flags may bear the arms of the see, the emblems of the patron saint, or the cross of St. George on a white ground, and in the first quarter a shield bearing the arms of the see in which the church is situated.

Pope Leo x (De'Medici) 1513

Cardinal Antonio Sanseverini, 1527

Fig. 97.

Or, five balls in orle gules, in chief a larger one of the arms of France: azure three fleurs-de-lis or

## Roman Catholic Church

The arms of the Pope are ensigned with the tiara. The tiara is a cap of metal or cloth of gold encircled with three open crowns of gold, foliated and enriched with pearls; the top is surmounted by an orb and a cross paty (Fig. 97).

The keys of St. Peter, gold on the dexter, silver on the sinister, are placed in saltire behind the shield.

An archbishop or bishop of the Roman Catholic Church may impale his personal arms with those of his see and if he is a cardinal he may place his scarlet hat above the shield with its tasselled pendants hanging down on each side (Fig. 97). The ecclesiastical hat of a cardinal is scarlet and that of an archbishop and bishop is green in colour. The number of tassels or houppes on their cords, pendant from either side of the hat, has varied from time to time; it is usual for those of a cardinal to number fifteen on either side arranged in pyramidal form with 5 in the bottom row and 4, 3, 2, 1, above; those of an archbishop number ten on either side arranged 4, 3, 2, 1, and for a bishop six on either side arranged 3, 2, 1.

An archbishop or bishop may ensign his arms with a mitre and crozier. The precious mitre, set with gem stones, is used only by those of episcopal rank, otherwise all are identical in form.

The following books contain useful information:

*Ecclesiastical Heraldry.* J. Woodward. 1894

*The Blazon of Episcopacy.* 2nd Edition. W. K. P. Bedford. 1897

*Papal Heraldry.* D. L. Galbreath. Cambridge. 1930

*Coutumes et Droit Héraldiques de l'Eglise.* Mgr. B. B. Heim. Beauchesne. 1949

# PART THREE

## HERALDIC DESIGN
### *'A Sense of Period'*

It has been well said that the development of heraldic draughtsmanship belongs to the history of decorative art, as it is distinct from the composition of arms which is the province of heralds.

Generally speaking heraldic design moves with the main stream of taste in its period, but being strongly traditional in character is less swayed by fashion than the other applied arts.

Through the centuries the College of Arms, being (the Crown excepted) the sole authority in England with power to act in regard to arms, the Kings of Arms, who are the granting authority, have not encouraged their own herald painters to experiment in style and this has had a stabilizing but limiting effect on heraldic design; even today some people believe that it is necessary to copy absolutely the pictorial designs made at the College but this is of course not true. The blazon must be correctly interpreted and where there is ambiguity the heralds are the interpreting authority, but the actual style of representation is the designer's own province.

Little is known about individual herald painters before the 19th century; each artist has interpreted blazons in accord with the fashion of his time and these differing manners have been equally correct heraldically, although some have had a higher standard of design than others. It is doubtful taste for an artist to take the shield of one period, typical charges of another and the helm and mantling of a third and mix them together in one design. A knowledge of styles of different periods is important, then if a period flavour is required the whole achievement may be designed in keeping—Medieval, Tudor, Restoration or Victorian as the case may be. Heraldic design is at its best, however, when it is a lively and fresh version of blazon designed in the idiom of its own day and 'avoids the hidebound pedantry which has done so much to narrow the art of heraldry.'

Beginning in the first half of the feudal 12th century, heraldry developed its characteristic picture language during the next two centuries and many people think the designer craftsmen of the 13th and 14th centuries remain unsurpassed, although, except for Mathew Paris, their names are unknown.

Heraldry on the battlefield was a simple and practical system of identification. Later the emphasis shifted to decorative display with the widespread use of heraldry in tournaments. Heraldic art followed the changed use and developed in richness and complexity during the age of chivalry.

During the 15th century the system became more elaborately organized and records and registrations of arms were kept by the Heralds. The granting of arms increased and also their fantastication. The Tudors loved colour and decorative show and few buildings of that period are without exemplification of arms. Much of the heraldry familiar to us comes from the Tudor and Stuart use of it with increasing elaboration and flamboyance of style. The Jacobean was an age of ostentation and some of the uses of heraldry, especially on small objects such as silver and rings, may have been responsible for the modern use of the term 'crest' instead of 'arms'.

In contrast to the magnificence of this display the actual composition of arms tended to be simple during the 17th century. In the 18th century a change in taste led to the granting of pictorial arms which were unheraldic and inimical to good design. The style of shield shapes, charges and crests, is influenced by the taste of the period in which they are current; exemplified by the Kings of Arms who are themselves influenced by the prevailing style in architecture and ornament. Victorian heraldry for example has been quoted by Sir Anthony Wagner as reflecting the overcrowded drawing-rooms of the Victorian era.

A fashion for heraldic stationery persisted through the 19th century and crests were engraved on notepaper, silver and signet rings. Arms with mean and naturalistic little charges appeared on bookplates and the like. At the end of the century William Morris, the reformer of applied design, among his many influences exerted a beneficial effect on heraldic draughtsmanship and encouraged people to look at design with new eyes, as he did also in the field of book production. At the beginning of the 20th century Oswald Barron exerted a reforming influence on heraldry and genealogy and rekindled admiration for medieval work, as did W. H. St. John Hope.

Although excellent work has been done by individual and anonymous craftsmen from late Tudor until Victorian times, on the whole the standard of design declined disastrously through the whole period. Artists today owe much to A. W. Pugin, Dom Anselm Baker, J. Forbes Nixon, E. E. Dorling, G. W. Eve and Kruger Gray who raised the standard of heraldic design in the late 19th and the early years of this century. In more recent years the work of Gerald Cobb, senior Herald Painter at the College of Arms, deserves to be more widely known, it owes its excellence, particularly as regards his rendering of lions, helms and mantlings, to a scholarly regard for historic examples. His designs for the illustrations appearing in Wagner's 'Historic Heraldry of Britain' are particularly commended for study.

## DESIGNING AN ACHIEVEMENT OF ARMS

The first essential of heraldic design is that it should be accurate. The value of a design is lost if it is not a true version of blazon. Heraldry has a message to convey and the forms must be recognizable if they are to have any meaning at all. Consequently the designer must take the trouble to make himself familiar with the basic grammar and rules of heraldry.

Heraldic design is not an original but an interpretative art. The designer is responsible for a good design but the components of it are not under his control, he has to make the best use of the many small parts as specified in the blazon. The test of his craftsmanship lies in reconciling these different, and sometimes incompatible units, into a well poised and vigorous whole. Discrepancies in the blazon should be checked by going back to the earliest authoritative sources. This research is not usually the province of artists. The majority of commissions for heraldic work consist of well-known coats of arms.

The designer should be able to draw objects and living creatures as the range of heraldry is wide. But even more important than skilled draughtsmanship, however, is the ability to plan a good design. This is based on a sense of balance between parts, a realization that the task is to blend the crest, a three-dimensional object, with the shield of two dimensions. The feeling for the push and pull of the abstract lines of the composition, the thrust of diagonals, the weight of verticals, the stability of horizontals and the like are of paramount importance. It is an excellent training for a designer to study fine work from the outstanding periods of historical heraldry in order to learn the rules and understand the insignia. 'Draughtsmen in the 13th century had often at once a freshness and a majesty of sight and touch now seldom seen', as Sir Anthony Wagner writes in 'Heraldry in England'.

It is of course bad practice, as has been said before, to mix styles of different historical periods or slavishly to copy exactly the painting in a grant of arms.

There is still a widespread belief that the style of painting in a grant of arms is sacrosanct and it must again be emphasized that this is not a fact. If this unlucky misconception could be overcome, heraldic artists and craftsmen would feel free to plan a coat of arms with more independence of spirit in the design and in the treatment of it.

The College of Arms is the immediate authority in matters of heraldry in England and the interpretation of blazon, but the College is not the arbiter of the aesthetics of heraldry. The naturalistic, rather pedestrian style of painting in grants at some periods need not be followed by designers of more abstract and adventurous inclinations.

The purpose of the design is one of the first considerations in planning the layout —whether it is small in scale and detailed as for an engraved bookplate, or bold and eye-catching, an inn sign or wrought iron gates for instance. The shape to be filled depends on the purpose and the medium. Armorial bearings can be so planned as to fill almost any shape, but overcrowding should be avoided. A full achievement of shield, helm and crest, one above the other, tends to fill an upright rectangle. If there are supporters the natural shape is a horizontal rectangle. Insignia also fit well into a roundel as on a seal or a boss. A lozenge is a decorative shape but difficult to fill comfortably. The parts of an achievement should be compact. If the spaces between the units are too widely separated, especially between the shield and its supporters, the design will tend to fall apart. The charges on the shield should occupy slightly less in area than the field surrounding them. The shape of the space available may require the crest to be exaggerated, or the shield may bear quarterings and so need to be enlarged in proportion in order to contain all the charges.

The aim is to display the arms clearly and the lines of helm, mantling and motto should direct attention to the shield and its charges and not distract from it.

The normal placing of shield, helm and crest is the natural one—as may be seen from the representations on early seals of armed knights on horseback (Plate 1, Fig. 1). In early manuscripts there are drawings of ceremonial occasions when the crested helm and its mantling were borne aloft on a lance shaft, the shield hanging below by its guige.

The designer can change this normal arrangement to suit his purpose—the shield may be placed beside the helm and crest or a coronet below it; supporters may hold the shield above their heads instead of at shoulder level.

Although extravagant arrangements are best avoided by the beginner in heraldic design (Fig. 61), there is scope for new layouts which preserve dignity and poise. If space is limited it is preferable to show the shield alone rather than a full achievement, if the latter would cause the charges to be rendered too small to be legible.

The arms and the crest may be borne together or separately and without helm, mantling, supporters or motto. If the crest is used alone, which should not be encouraged, it should be shown standing on a crest wreath. If the arms are used alone they may fill a shape other than that of a shield.

It has been well said that heraldry is 'vulnerable to ridicule', and as it is often

Fig. 98. The Royal Arms.   1799

Fig. 99. The Royal Arms.   1851 Exhibition

used to enhance feelings of tradition and prestige any design which inadvertently makes it appear ridiculous destroys its purpose.   The serious designer (as opposed to the intentionally flippant, Fig. 98) should aim at dignity and vitality and so avoid being open to such a criticism as this: 'Heraldic forms in most unheraldic attitudes dodge round weakly designed shields, from above which tiny coronets topple, quite regardless of the balanced composition of good design.' Thus G. W. Eve writing about 19th-century heraldic art in 'Decorative Heraldry' (Fig. 99).

Our century has more sympathy for abstract design than the last, and so it should be easier for designers to free themselves from naturalism and return to a more stylized rendering of the creatures of heraldry. This stylization should convey that sense of meaning which is the characteristic of enduring symbols. The heraldic lion is a different beast from a living lion. He is the abstract expression of a lion's attributes of nobility, power, strength, courage, vitality and ferocity. These qualities should animate the design of nearly all heraldic animals and monsters. The flowing line down the spine and hindquarters can be made to express this life and the massive shoulders and strong forelegs should give a sense of power; the unsheathed claws and open jaws express ferocity. The tail should spring from the loins and the hair from the tail with a similar spirit. The lines of the mantling can be made to echo the liveliness of the supporters and add to the life of the design. While the formal elements of heraldry commonly give dignity and symmetry, the beasts, objects, and mantling are the opportunity to express vitality and rhythm.

One should avoid flaccid drawing, weak curves, fussy mantling and fubsy or pet-like animals. The eyes of these animals are better when set high in the skull, as this will avoid the puppyish look and for the same reason, the nose should be long and haughty rather than snub like a Teddy Bear.

Although the limitations of much heraldic art are stringent, interpretation is possible in an interesting range of methods, styles and materials.

Gold, silver and vivid colours are an integral part of heraldry as a system, but much sound designing has been done in line and monochrome. A design may be conceived in white outline and texture, as on sandblasted glass for decorative windows or panels, and these are dramatic when edge lit. A white line is also used in engraving on wood, glass and silver, examples of which are shown in the illustrations.

A black line is used in most graphic design for reproduction, and in pierced or wrought iron work. Heraldry in monochrome also looks well in natural stone or wood, whether flat in treatment or carved in varying degrees of relief, in paper sculpture, cut metal foil and solid and translucent plastics, which have also been used for display work. When heraldry on a flat surface is designed in full colour emphasis may still be chiefly linear. Heraldry in colour can also be treated as absolutely flat pattern, or painted to imitate modelling, and modelled heraldry may in turn be painted. A coat of arms can be rendered as a mosaic of bright colours and metals of different tones; or unified by a low, nearly even, tone of different colours to show up against a light background.

Heraldic designs may be embroidered in silk or wool, or appliquéd in differently textured stuffs.   The methods are as extensive as the range of materials, and all these different media require a fresh approach in the making of the design.   A versatile designer should be able to interpret the heraldry to suit both the material in which it is to be displayed and the scale of the work.   A craftsman specializing in one particular material would do well to master the application of heraldic design to his craft.

# A METHOD OF WORKING

The arms of the Westminster City Council have been chosen as the subject of this description of the author's method of making a straightforward heraldic design in black and white.   The arms exhibit an interesting variety of charges which also have historical associations, and the lion supporters are both charged and collared.

Fig. 100.

The Preliminary Sketch

## The Preliminary Sketch

Firstly the blazon was studied and visualized with the aid of the 'tricks' made from the records at the College of Arms (Fig. 8a, b).

In making the sketch the base line AB and the centre vertical CD were set out (Fig. 100).   A heater shaped shield was sketched freehand and the charges indicated summarily.   The idea of a shield couché, i.e. tilting to the dexter, was discarded as the charge of a portcullis requires to be upright. The helm and crest were lightly plotted thus establishing the height of the drawing. The supporters were indicated diagramatically thus giving its approximate width. The horizontal motto scroll with swallowtail ends served as a base line for the design. The main curves of the mantling were sketched in the upper quarters of the rectangle. The natural shape of this achievement was obviously a horizontal one but for the purpose of a book illustration an upright rectangle seemed preferable, accordingly a rectangle of proportions better suited to the shape of the page was drawn and made one-third larger than the size the reproduced drawing (see page 18) was to be. A centre line and diagonals were indicated as aids to symmetry and construction (Fig. 101).

Fig. 101.

The Working Drawing

## The Working Drawing: The Relation of Parts to the Whole

The satisfactory designing of heraldry depends on the relation of parts to the whole. The medieval herald painters in a simple arrangement of shield, helm and

29*a*. Royal Arms displayed by a Royal Warrant Holder.   Top left, by appointment to Her Majesty Queen Elizabeth II; top right, by appointment to the late King George VI; below, by appointment to H.R.H. the Prince of the Netherlands

Arms of the Worshipful Company of Leathersellers' on entrance gates to the Livery Hall

29*c*. Arms of the Hudson Bay Company in plaster on the ceiling of the gateway into Leathersellers' Hall

30a. One of six claret jugs engraved with the arms of the Worshipful Company of Saddlers', by Stephen Rickard

30b. Decanter engraved with the arms of Hesketh of North Meols by Laurence Whistler. Note the addition of emblems personal to Lady Mary Hesketh for whom the decanter was engraved

30c. The Royal Arms and the arms of the Heralds attending the coronation of Her Majesty Queen Elizabeth II, diamond-point engraving on a Whitefriars glass plate by Sheila Elmhirst

*a.* Arms of the Worshipful Company of Clothworkers' designed Hugh Easton for a stained glass window in the Livery Hall. e shields below display the arms of Shearmen and Fullers pectively before their union in 1510 as the Clothworkers

31*b.* Arms of Henry Godolphin from one of a series of eight stained glass windows each containing four coats of arms, designed by Miss Moira Forsyth for Eton College Chapel

32a. Arms of the Royal Society commissioned by [the] Society to commemorate the tercentenary, with the a[rms] of the founder below and the present patron abo[ve.] Designed by William Gardner and executed at the Wh[ite]friars Stained Glass Studios

32b. Lions, unicorns, crowns and banners floodlit. The Mall, coronation of H.M. Queen Elizabeth II. *Crown Copyright*

crest made the proportion of the shield about two-fifths of the total height; the helm and crest being rather less than three-fifths.   A generally satisfactory alternative and the one adopted here, is to make the helm and crest together nearly the same height as the shield.   The proportions may also be planned on a practical basis so that the bearer of the shield could actually wear the size of helm and crest represented in the design.

## Shape of Shield

The first sketch had demonstrated that a heater shape did not allow sufficient space for the chains of the portcullis.   Consequently a squarer form of shield was chosen in the working drawing.

## Charges

The proportion of the chief to the field was indicated, i.e. rather less than one-third.   The charges were symmetrically arranged and their sizes established.

## Crest and Helm

The crest and helm were considered together.   In civic heraldry it is usual for an esquire's helm to be used to support the crest.   The crest, a portcullis flanked on each side by a rose, stalked, leaved and erect, gives an impression of weight and requires the support of a sturdy helm, of the type used in tournaments, placed centrally on top of the shield.   The strong diagonal thrust of the front edge of the helm is helpful in leading the eye to the vertical and horizontal lines of the shield and crest.   In itself, however, the crest of a portcullis is not happily chosen, as it lacks roundness; to marry it to the helm in such a way that it looks as if actually modelled (as it would have to be if it were atop a memorial slab or sculpted in any medium) the portcullis needs to be put into three-quarter perspective, with the helm in similar perspective, for otherwise if shown like a comb standing across the helm from front to rear, all that would be seen from directly in front or behind would be a thin iron rod standing erect obscured by a rose climbing up it.

## Proportions

As the height of the crest and helm together approximates to that of the shield, the relative proportions of these items places the helm just above the middle of the whole group where it becomes a focal point around which the other important parts of the achievement are composed.

KHD

## Supporters

The supporters were sketched next into the space available on each side of the shield. There is less freedom of movement for them here than in the preliminary sketch, but if compactly placed and drawn in a spirited manner they give stability to the design. They should not be too large or they dwarf the shield, or so small that they cannot see one another across the top of it, or require to stand on tiptoe in order to do so.

## The Compartment

or mount, on which the supporters stand, generally called the compartment, and the motto and the scroll on which it is written, were designed as a whole, the three words of the motto made a symmetrical arrangement possible.

## Charges

The charges were next considered in detail (Fig. 102); firstly the charge on the field of the shield itself; the bars of the portcullis were drawn to make the spaces between them a square; the links in the chain were drawn in a related, angular style, and a ring was attached to the end of each chain. The cross flory on the pale in chief was drawn with equal arms; the five martlets were arranged around it, space being allowed for one of them under the base of the cross. The Tudor roses on the chief were designed geometrically, as is the heraldic convention for roses and the barbs and seeds were added.

## Crest

The crest was considered in detail with its single roses—these were more freely drawn than the Tudor roses in the arms, but still treated in the conventional terms; they stand erect on either side of the portcullis, barbed, seeded, stalked and leaved. They need not be identical, and are best shown varying in plane to the portcullis.

## Crest Wreath

The crest wreath surrounding the base of the crest was drawn so that it appears firmly pressed down on the brow of the helm, the separate twists of the cloth showing clearly the six pieces, alternately or and azure, beginning on the dexter side with the metal and finishing on the sinister with the colour.

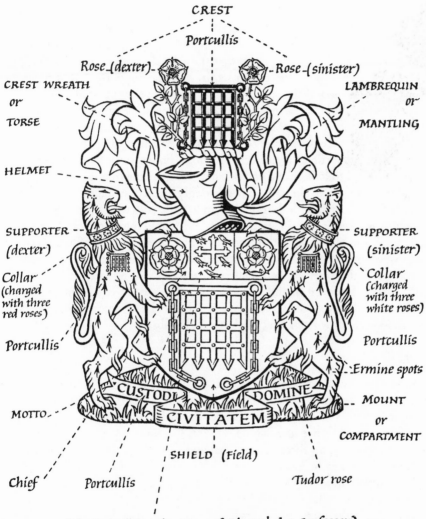

CREST

Portcullis

Rose (dexter)

Rose (sinister)

CREST WREATH or TORSE

LAMBREQUIN or MANTLING

HELMET

SUPPORTER (dexter)

SUPPORTER (sinister)

Collar (charged with three red roses)

Collar (charged with three white roses)

Portcullis

Portcullis

Ermine spots

MOTTO

Mount or COMPARTMENT

CUSTODI DOMINE CIVITATEM

Chief

Portcullis

SHIELD (Field)

Tudor rose

Pale (containing the arms of Edward the Confessor)

ARMS OF THE CITY OF WESTMINSTER

Fig. 102.

## Supporters

The treatment of the supporters was taken next. Their limbs were deliberately and naturally arranged so as to support the shield in a vigorous manner without extravagant gesture. Care was taken that they should not obscure the charges on the shield or the words on the motto-scroll. Similar supporters need not appear identical on either side of the shield they support, the easy method is to trace one and reverse it for the other; a more lively approach is to design each separately and balance one with the other. Supporters are not subject to the same restrictions in attitude as charges. To give variety to the design the sinister supporter may hold the helm as well as supporting the shield. The lions' bodies are slightly attenuated, the heads are intended to look proud and defiant. A firm line runs down the spine and rear leg of each animal, the tail grows strongly from the spine. The toes were drawn widely separated with the claws extended; the jaws wide open and the tongue thrust out; the expressions aim to be fierce and feline, but not grotesque; and the eyes are small and placed high in the head. The manes and tufts of hair on the tails and legs were treated in the heraldic convention. The shoulders and the body had to be wide enough to carry the portcullis charge as if the same were branded thereon and not merely stuck on in the same plane or by way of extension of the two-dimensional rendering of the same device in the shield, and according to the blazon ermine spots were powdered over the body and limbs.

## Collars

The perspective of the collars was given careful thought; in heraldic design even a slightly concave or convex curve in such small items as collars, crest wreaths, coronets and scrolls can change the balance of a design and add or detract from its coherence as a whole.

The supporters being three dimensional and hence capable of recognition from every angle, it cannot be assumed that the roses on the collars could only be seen from one flank—these should be drawn as if placed evenly like studs all round and not just on one side of the collars—an example of the necessity of sometimes having to ignore the literal blazon (which often disregards the 'roundness' of supporters or crest) in order to make a logical design.

## Mantling

The balance of the mantling in a black and white line drawing is simpler than in a coloured design. It is in the decorative handling of mantling that the skill of the designer is really called into play. The strong twists and flourishes of the material as it flows out from under the crest wreath can invigorate the design. Mantling that is weak or limp, starched into stiff folds, or broken into meaningless pieces of colour and metal is seldom as effective as a material that appears to flow in three-dimensional curves.

## The Compartment

Finally the detailed treatment of the ground on which the shield and the supporters stand was considered. In this specimen design short tufts of grass have been used to make a texture on the mound. The motto scroll is not tapered, it is equal in width throughout its length, the slight thickness of the ribbon is shown along the top edge to give a feeling of solidity.

## Inking in

The whole design having been drawn lightly in pencil the outline of the shield was then established with ruler and pen compass. The remainder of the design was painted with a brush and ivory-black water colour. The outlines of the main parts of the design on the whole were made stronger than the lines used for the details inside the forms. A pen and black ink could have been used instead of a brush and paint, and would have been better had the drawing been intended for reproduction on a much reduced scale.

The degree of finish and the amount of elaboration which should be included in a painting of an achievement depends on the size and character of the work and the purpose for which it is intended. It can be a waste of time to put elaborate detail into a painting that is to be reproduced, for much of it may be lost in the process of reproduction. On the other hand in a unique work, such as an illumination on vellum, a high degree of finish and fine detail is appropriate. In paintings on a small scale it may be sufficient to paint a firm outline round charges and supporters, after the shapes have been laid in with flat colour; but on a larger scale the same shapes may appear too empty and flat without some indication of modelling on them.

The outline round shield and charges, whether it is made with strong strokes of the brush, pen, chisel or graver, should always be firm and expressive. The outline should never have about it a broken or tentative look.

On the whole the modelling on objects, on animals, and on drapery should be treated in a broad and simplified manner, with the careful placing of a few lines to represent the mane or muscles of a lion, or folds on drapery, rather than an attempt at realistic shading in tone, or by means of cross hatching.

In painting charges on a shield, it should be noted that the effect of a charge that is light in colour on a dark field, or vice versa, is to alter the apparent size of the charge. When a strong outline is used round charges allowance must also be made for the tendency that the outline will merge into the darker of the two tinctures; in each case the object will need to be drawn slightly larger or smaller as the case may be. Charges should never be rendered in such high relief that they appear to be detached from the field of the shield.

---

In the following pages the four illustrations show variations in the insignia and accessories that may be encountered in designing an achievement of arms of a peer of the realm, a baronet, a Knight of the Garter and an esquire.

Fig. 103. The Arms
of Viscount Nuffield

VISCOUNT NUFFIELD

## A PEER OF THE REALM

The Viscount Nuffield.   Sir William Richard Morris, O.B.E., of Nuffield, Oxford,
and a Baronet (Fig. 103).

BLAZON

ARMS: *Ermine, on a fesse or, between in chief two roses gules, barbed and seeded proper, and
in base a balance of the second, three pears sable.*

CREST: *A demi-bull gules, armed and unguled or, resting the sinister hoof on a winged wheel
or.*

SUPPORTERS: *On either side a beaver vert, the tail scaly argent and azure, gorged with a
collar pendent therefrom an escutcheon or charged with three pears slipped sable.*

BADGE: Two sprigs of speedwell in saltire enfiled with a viscount's coronet proper
(Fig. 81*i*).                                      MOTTO: Fiat justitia.

A shield with a broad base was chosen to take the width of the scales in the base. The ermine tails were plotted symmetrically over the entire field before the fesse and the charges were drawn on it.

The coronet of a viscount, showing nine of its sixteen silver balls on a circlet, was placed centrally on top of the shield. The coronet was represented here without the cap inside.

The peer's helm of silver, barred and decorated with gold, was set sideways above and within the coronet. The crest, a demi-bull, rests its sinister hoof on a winged wheel, an emblem of strength and speed. (That the creature is not blazoned as a demi-ox is a curious vagary of the granting authorities.)

The beavers with their scaly tails represent industry and the river-waters of Oxford, and from their collars hang escutcheons charged with three pears placed two and one. To the purist this must be bad heraldry, for thereby is created a new coat of arms, of pears, outside the medium of the main shield: to make a shield shape other than the main shield into a vehicle for the display of charges is to be deplored on this account. If the whole arms were to be displayed on these lesser shields there would be less objection, though how a shield pendant from a supporter's collar can magnetize itself to a spectator's field of vision whatever his standpoint is hard to understand—and if it does not, then these beavers as supporters are hardly distinguishable from other beavers as supporters in other arms.

The badge, punning on Lord Nuffield's career, shows crossed sprigs of speedwell surrounded with a viscount's coronet; the plant is depicted on the mound in this drawing.

The arms of Lord Nuffield have been granted to Nuffield College, Oxford, by Royal Licence (Plate 21c).

Arms of a Baronet
Sir James Edmund
Henderson NEVILLE, Bt.

A Baronet's helm is
similar to that of an
Esquire but it is borne
full faced with the
vizor raised.

Baronets bear as an
augmentation the
Badge of Ulster; an
inescutcheon argent
charged with a sinister
hand gules.

Fig. 104.

# A BARONET

Sir James Edmund Henderson Neville, Baronet, of Sloley, Norfolk (Fig. 104).

BLAZON

ARMS: *Sable, a chevron invected vair between three lions rampant or, each holding between the paws an escutcheon argent charged with an eagle's head erased azure.*

CREST: *An eagle displayed sable, upon the breast and each wing an escutcheon or, charged with a lion's head erased also sable.*

MOTTO: Vitam impendere vero.

The distinguishing badge of a baronet, the red hand of Ulster on a white ground, is borne as an escutcheon on the arms; it is placed centrally on the chief where it does not obscure the charges. The lions above the chevron were designed in this drawing to hold their shields between their paws with the tops of the shields on a level with one another, their limbs have been arranged to fit the shapes in which they have to be placed and so the lion in the base is slightly larger than the other two. The chevron is invected, with the points turning inwards, and the early form of vair has been used in this drawing.

The steel helm of a baronet is borne full faced with the visor raised, the crest wreath appears encircling the brow of the helm behind the visor, and the scarlet silk of the padded lining shows within the helm.

The eagle crest is charged with three escutcheons which have all been made the same size, the two on the wings being level with one another. The tail of the eagle rests on the helm and the claws straddle the crest wreath. The lions' heads on the escutcheons in the crest and the eagles' heads on the escutcheons in the arms are all erased.

The mantling of sable lined argent was designed so that the silvery lining flanks the shield, thus avoiding the confusion of sable mantling with the sable field.

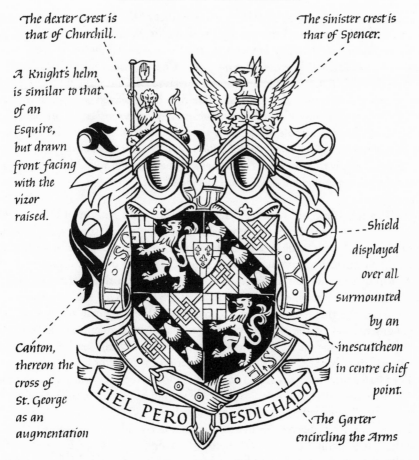

*The dexter Crest is that of Churchill.*

*The sinister crest is that of Spencer.*

*A Knight's helm is similar to that of an Esquire, but drawn front facing with the vizor raised.*

*Shield displayed over all surmounted by an inescutcheon in centre chief point.*

*Canton, thereon the cross of St. George as an augmentation*

*The Garter encircling the Arms*

FIEL PERO DESDICHADO

*Arms of Sir Winston* CHURCHILL, *Knight of the Garter*

**Fig. 105.**

# A KNIGHT OF THE GARTER

Rt. Hon. Sir Winston Leonard Spencer Churchill, K.G., O.M., C.H. (Fig. 105). The shield shows in the first and fourth quarters the arms of CHURCHILL: *Sable a lion rampant argent with a canton of the last thereon a cross gules;* the cross of St. George was granted as an augmentation to the first Sir Winston Churchill, the father of the first Duke of Marlborough, in recognition of his services to King Charles I as Captain of the Horse, and his loyalty to Charles II as a Member of the House of Commons. In the second and third quarters are the arms of Sir Winston Churchill's paternal family of SPENCER: *Quarterly argent and gules, in the second and third quarters a fret or, over all a bend sable three escallops of the first.* George, fifth Duke of Marlborough, was empowered to assume the additional surname of Churchill with his paternal coat of Spencer. He was also granted a shield to be displayed over all in the centre chief point: *Argent a cross of St. George surmounted by an inescutcheon azure charged with three fleurs-de-lis or.* The dexter crest is that of Churchill: *A lion couchant guardant argent supporting a banner gules charged with a dexter hand couped of the first, staffed or.* The sinister crest is that of Spencer: *Out of a coronet a griffin's head between two wings expanded argent gorged with a collar gemel and armed gules.*

Sir Winston Churchill's arms are shown as those of a Knight of the Garter and his other Orders are therefore omitted. The display of these quartered arms required a shield with straight sides and a wide base, the top and sides of the shield were slightly curved to give it more elegance. The size of the cantons in the first and fourth quarters was not allowed to obscure more than the dexter foreleg of the lion rampant. The second and third quarters are themselves quartered and on the bend overall the three escallops are placed along the diagonal and not across it. The augmentation of the shield overall was placed in the centre chief point; this shield had to be large enough to show the inescutcheon with the three fleurs-de-lis, but not so large that it would obscure the charges in the arms.

The Garter surrounds the shield and was made appreciably wider than the motto scroll which forms the base line. The shield should be set inside the Garter and not appear to be slipping out of it, as is sometimes seen.

Two crests are displayed on helms placed side by side on the top of the shield with the Garter behind them. The helm of a knight as that of a baronet is of steel with the visor raised and shown front facing, inside the padded silk of the lining can be seen. The brow of the dexter helm is encircled with a crest wreath, the sinister with a ducal coronet. The problem of the adjustment of the crest to helm has been discussed under CRESTS in this book. Here the lion couchant appears astride the dexter helm and looks startled to find himself and the banner he is holding, travelling in a different direction from the helm. However, he is in good company, as the Royal Crest is in like condition as regards its affronty Sovereign's helm. With the Churchill crest it is also to be assumed that some convenient wind will keep the banner constantly to the spectator's line of vision. It is suggested that to incorporate a banner, bearing a charge, in a Crest is poor composition and there are indications that such crests would not be granted today. In the sinister crest the head only of the griffin is turned to the dexter, the wings and breast are in line with the helm.   This crest is gorged with a collar of narrow twin bars.   It would be permissible to turn the helms slightly to the side and the crests also, but neither in this case would make the dexter crest convincing, it would require the helm to be completely side facing.   In the circumstances this abandonment of the position rules for helms would be justified, since whatever position it holds, a knight's helm is always recognizable as such by its distinctive open visor.

The tinctures of the mantling on the two helmets is different: that on the dexter is sable doubled argent; on the sinister gules doubled argent.   In order to avoid overcrowding the design the mantling between the two helms was made very short, but on the outside it was allowed to sweep down the sides and curl through the space between the shield and the Garter.

## THE ARMS OF AN ESQUIRE

Michael Charles St. John Hornby, Esquire (Fig. 106).

**BLAZON**

ARMS: *Argent, a chevron vert, in base a bugle-horn stringed sable, on a chief of the second, two bugle-horns of the field.*

CREST: *A bugle-horn stringed sable and passing through the knot in fesse an arrow point towards the sinister, or.*

MOTTO: Crede Cornu.

HORNBY
Fig. 106.

This is an attractive example of a canting or punning coat displaying the comparatively unusual colour green. The two ordinaries and the three similar charges require nice adjustment in their proportions, while they allow a tapering elegant form of shield to be used. The three horns in the arms are not exact copies of one another, there is room for the horn in the base to be slightly larger than the two in chief.

The esquire's steel helm, which is closed, is set sideways on the top of the shield. The bugle-horn in the crest is also seen in profile although it is given some solidity. The blazon indicates both the tincture and the direction in which the arrow points, the knot of sable strings holds it in a totally unrealistic and horizontal position above the horn.

In keeping with the charges and colours evocative of woodlands and hunting the windswept mantling is serrated into leaf-shapes with marked centre ribs.

The motto ribbon reflects the curve of the horn and joins with the mantling to enclose the design. The two words of the motto permit the shield to overlap the scroll in the centre with one word on each side. It is seldom satisfactory to design the shield so that the point of it just touches the edge of the scroll, as this makes a visually uncomfortable point, called a 'false centre', on which the shield may inadvertently appear to rock.

Fig. 107. Royal Arms designed by Reynolds Stone for the War Graves Commission. Reproduced by permission of the Controller of H.M. Stationery Office

## ROYAL HERALDRY OF GREAT BRITAIN

The Royal Arms are Arms of Dominion and Sovereignty. They are borne by kings and queens by virtue of their high office and as emblems of authority which are only affected by dynastic change. In the United Kingdom, as in many other countries of Europe, the Royal Arms are also regarded as arms of the State.

The Royal Arms (Fig. 107) have undergone many changes through the centuries and in their present form they date from the accession of Queen Victoria in 1837; they consist of:

THE ARMS: *Quarterly 1 and 4. Gules, three lions passant guardant or, for England. 2. Or, a lion rampant within a double tressure fleury counterfleury gules, for Scotland. 3. Azure, a harp or, stringed argent, for Ireland.* The shield is encircled with the Garter.

CREST: *Upon the Royal Helm the Royal Crown proper, thereon a lion statant guardant or, royally crowned proper.*

MANTLING: *Gold lined with ermine.*

SUPPORTERS: *Dexter, a lion guardant or, royally crowned proper. Sinister, a unicorn argent, armed, crined and unguled or, gorged with a coronet of fleurs-de-lis and crosses paty a chain affixed thereto passing between the fore-legs and reflexed over the back, or.*

MOTTO: Dieu et mon Droit.

BADGES (Fig. 82): *The red and white rose united, slipped and leaved proper*—England. *A thistle slipped and leaved proper*—Scotland. *A shamrock leaf slipped vert*—Ireland. *A harp or, stringed argent*—Ireland. The rose, thistle and shamrock engrafted on one stem, proper—the United Kingdom. *An escutcheon charged with the Union Flag*—the United Kingdom. All these badges are ensigned with the Royal Crown. Wales—*within a circular band argent fimbriated or bearing the motto 'Y ddraig goch ddyry cychwyn', in letters vert, and ensigned with the Royal Crown proper an escutcheon per fesse argent and vert and thereon the Red Dragon passant.* The emblems of Wales are the leek, and the daffodil, of more recent provenance as such.

## Form of the Royal Arms adopted in Scotland

From the beginnings of heraldry Scotland has always had its own Royal Arms; the lion rampant within a tressure ornamented with fleurs-de-lis appears on the great seal of King Alexander II dated 1222. The English arrangement of the Royal Arms made after the union of the Crowns in 1603 was not accepted in Scotland. The achievement of the Royal Arms of Great Britain as officially used in Scotland is: *Quarterly, 1 and 4. The Royal Arms of Scotland. 2. The Royal Arms of England. 3. The Royal Arms of Ireland. Around the shield is the collar of the Most Ancient and Most Noble Order of the Thistle, with the Badge of St. Andrew pendent therefrom.* Crest (Fig. 108): *On an Imperial Crown proper, a lion sejant affronty gules, armed and langued azure, crowned, holding in the dexter paw a sword and in the sinister paw a sceptre, both proper, and on a scroll over the same the motto: 'In defens'.* Supporters: *On a compartment, with the motto, 'Nemo Me Impune Lacessit', are set, dexter, the unicorn, crowned, and sinister, the lion guardant, the former sustaining a banner emblazoned azure a saltire argent, the latter a banner emblazoned argent, a cross gules.*

## The Royal Arms in Northern Ireland

The Royal Arms used in Northern Ireland are the same as those used in England except that the crest of Ireland (Fig. 108)—a stag prancing out of a castle, which stands on a wreath—replaces the crest of England above the shield.

The Irish harp may be represented in a variety of forms; the Celtic harp and the 'winged figure' are two versions (Fig. 108).

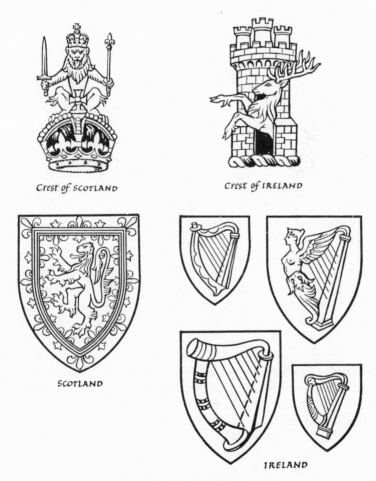

Crest of SCOTLAND

Crest of IRELAND

SCOTLAND

IRELAND

Fig. 108. Royal Heraldry of Great Britain

## Use of the Royal Arms

The Royal Arms may be displayed only by the ruling Sovereign, by departments and officers of the Government in their official capacity, and by such persons and bodies as have been granted a licence by the Sovereign to do so. Permission to reproduce the Royal Arms in any form must be obtained from the Controller of H.M. Stationery Office, in which the Crown copyright is vested.

The Royal Arms are widely used and are familiar to most people in Great Britain. Her Majesty's Stationery Office use the arms in various forms on official documents and publications as in Figs. 107, 111, 112.

The arms encircled by the Garter, supported by the lion and unicorn and accompanied by the motto, proliferate in public, on Post Offices, post vans, and public buildings. Coins of the realm (Plate 22) display the arms on the reverse of the half-crown piece; on the crown piece the arms of England, Scotland and Ireland are shown on separate shields, with the rose, the thistle, the shamrock and the leek between them and the Royal Crown in the centre. The arms of England appear on the reverse of the English shilling, the arms of Scotland on the Scottish shillings, each surmounted with slightly different crowns. The florin bears a double rose within a wreath of thistles, shamrock and leeks, and these national emblems are also on the sixpence. The Tudor portcullis appears on the threepenny bit. The rose, thistle, shamrock and daffodil are also used on postage stamps.

Royal Warrant holders are granted the privilege of displaying the arms with the addition of the wording 'By Royal Appointment to . . .' on their business premises, shop fronts, vehicles, letterheads and the like (Plate 29). 'By appointment' packaging of goods is familiar to us all. Some of these designs of the Royal Arms are excellent, others are poor in both design and execution. The representations vary from carved achievements in the round, paintings on flat surfaces or in low relief, often richly enamelled, to small black and white designs suited to packaging or graphic reproduction.

The practice of displaying the Royal Arms in churches dating back to the reign of Henry VIII, makes these carved and painted arms an interesting study for the designer, since they reflect the changing taste in ornament at different periods. The majority date from the restoration of the monarchy and are not always correct in heraldic detail.

**MEMBERS OF THE ROYAL FAMILY**

Members of the Royal Family, other than the Sovereign, have their own arms, which are the Royal Arms with slight differences; they are not entitled to use the undifferenced Royal Arms.

ARMS OF H.R.H. THE DUKE OF EDINBURGH

Fig. 109.

HIS ROYAL HIGHNESS THE DUKE OF EDINBURGH bears for arms (Fig. 109) the four quarterings of Denmark, Greece, Mountbatten and the City of Edinburgh. The dexter supporter is Hercules from the Greek arms, the sinister is the Hesse lion gorged with a naval crown.

HER ROYAL HIGHNESS QUEEN ELIZABETH THE QUEEN MOTHER bears for arms those of the Sovereign impaling Bowes-Lyon.

LHD*

A full description of the arms of the Royal Family, the House of Windsor, with illustrations will be found in 'Burke's Peerage' and also in 'Debrett'.

Fig. 110. Royal Cipher designed by Reynolds Stone

Fig. 111. The Royal Arms designed by Reynolds Stone. Used on H.M. Stationery Office publications.

Fig. 112. The Royal Arms designed by Kruger Gray

These three designs reproduced by permission of the Controller of Her Majesty's Stationery Office

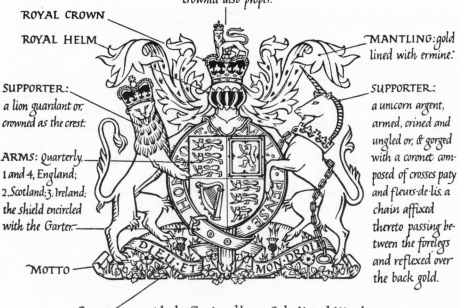

CREST
Upon the Royal helmet the Crown proper thereon a lion statant-guardant or, crowned also proper.

ROYAL CROWN

ROYAL HELM

MANTLING: gold lined with ermine.

SUPPORTER:
a lion guardant or, crowned as the crest.

SUPPORTER:
a unicorn argent, armed, crined and ungled or, & gorged with a coronet composed of crosses paty and fleurs-de-lis, a chain affixed thereto passing between the forelegs and reflexed over the back gold.

ARMS: Quarterly, 1 and 4, England; 2. Scotland; 3. Ireland; the shield encircled with the Garter.

MOTTO

Compartment with the floral emblems of the United Kingdom.

THE ROYAL ARMS

Fig. 113. The Royal Arms discussed in detail

# REPRESENTATIONS OF THE ROYAL ARMS

The insignia which are included in a representation of the Royal Arms will vary with the purpose and scale of the design. A design may consist of the arms encircled with the Garter and surmounted by the Crown only; in another the supporters and motto may be included as in Figs. 111, 112. A full achievement of the Royal Arms designed as a straightforward graphic representation is shown in Fig. 113 and discussed in detail (as this may be of help to other designers even when working in more elaborate media and in colours). The heraldic details will apply to any design.

*THE SHIELD:* The quartered shield is designed rather square and broad in the base. The gold lions passant guardant of England on a field gules are armed and langued azure. In the second quarter the lion rampant gules of Scotland on a gold ground is also armed and langued azure. It is important that the tressure with its alternating fleurs-de-lis should be shown double even on a small scale. In the third quarter the Irish harp, gold on an azure field, is normally represented with seven strings. The harp has assumed various forms since the arms of Ireland were introduced in the reign of James I; some of these variations are shown in Fig. 108.

The circlet surrounding the shield is a representation of the Garter, part of the insignia of the Most Noble Order of the Garter, of which the Sovereign is head. The Garter bears the motto 'Honi soit qui mal y pense' and these words should be spaced round the circle as if the letters were not hidden by the accessories. The letters, the edge of the circlet and the buckle are all gold on a deep blue ground. The pendant end having passed through the buckle turns over the circlet, the golden end of it may be ornamental and is sometimes represented as too large to pass through the buckle. The garter is usually drawn as a circle and while this is certainly easier for the designer as it can be struck with a compass, there are times when an oval may be preferable and this is a permissible variation (Fig. 72e).

THE HELM: The Sovereign's gold helm affronty, usually represented with an uneven number of bars across the face-piece, surmounts the shield and the Garter and from the top of the helm flows the mantling.

THE MANTLING: The mantling is gold lined with ermine, the ermine tails must be designed to follow the direction of the cloth and point towards the base of it. The mantling may end in golden tassels.

THE ROYAL CROWN (Fig. 76): The Crown surmounts the helm. It is the Crown of the United Kingdom and of all the other realms and territories of which Her Majesty Queen Elizabeth II is sovereign. It is not a personal device but a symbol of dominion inseparable from the rank and office of the Sovereign. In a design of the Royal Arms the Crown is represented in a conventional manner; it is not an exact likeness of an important part of the regalia. From time to time the conventional drawing of the Crown is altered and on the accession of Queen Elizabeth II the representation of the Crown was revised, it being ordained that the new design would be known as St. Edward's Crown.

The Crown is blazoned proper and it consists of a gold circlet jewelled with a ruby between two emeralds, with two sapphires showing at the edges, thereon four crosses paty (one and two halves being visible) and four fleurs-de-lis heads (two visible). The arches curve upwards and are slightly depressed where they meet in the centre, nine pearls are shown on each half of the complete arch, and five pearls are shown on the visible half of the second arch. In the centre where the arches meet the orb is placed; this consists of an emerald cross-banded with two gold fillets set with a ruby where the fillets meet and on either side three pearls are visible. The orb is surmounted by a cross paty gold. In early heraldry the cross paty was drawn with concave sides, which is more attractive than the straight-sided form often seen in modern manuals (Fig. 49*h*).

The cap is crimson velvet with the ermine lining appearing below the rim of the Crown.

*The Royal Arms and Badges*

Fig. 114. The Royal Arms designed to fill an elongated shape, freely adapted from 'Foster's Peerage', 1880

*THE CREST:* The lion statant guardant or stands upon the arches of the Crown, he is armed and langued gules, and the crown he wears is a replica of the crown on which he stands.

*THE SUPPORTERS:* On the dexter side the lion rampant guardant, symbol of power, should be drawn so as to express pride and defiance as he supports the Royal Arms. He is armed and langued gules and the Crown is tinctured proper as in the arms.

The supporter on the sinister, the unicorn argent, is a legendary beast. The first written descriptions of the unicorn date from 400 B.C. and through the ages he has symbolized many virtues; as supporter of the Royal Arms he should express dignity and strength. The unicorn is most satisfactory when designed as a slim creature with the lines of a race horse or gazelle; it looks clumsy when treated as a heavy animal such as a cart horse. The sharp twisted horn grows out of his forehead and this with the beard, mane and tufts of hair on limbs and tail are gold. The circle of the Royal coronet is gold and jewelled like the circle of the crowns, on the rim are four crosses paty (one and two halves visible) between four fleurs-de-lis heads (two visible). From the coronet hangs a chain of gold links ending in a ring. A test of a good designer is to make two dissimilar supporters balance one another in weight and proportion (Fig. 107).

*THE COMPARTMENT:* The green mound of grass on which the supporters stand may be decorated with the rose, thistle and shamrock emblems. The motto scroll may be designed in any way that suits the base of the design, the letters being gold on a pale blue ribbon edged with gold. The words 'Dieu et Mon Droit' are said to have been used by Richard I at the Battle of Gisors in 1190 with the meaning that the right to be king derived from God and not from France.

The full achievement of the Royal Arms has been described in detail here, but the artist must naturally use discretion as to how much detail to include in a design. For instance, the number of pearls in the crowns and strings on the harp cannot always be shown in full; on a very small scale a shorthand version has to be invented in drawing the lions and tressure in the arms. Clarity is more important than the inclusion of detail not essential to the correct interpretation of blazon. This of course applies to all forms of heraldic design, but clarity should not be sought for at the expense of technical accuracy.

Some recent modern versions of the Royal Arms although heraldically correct are grotesque in taste and unattractive in design.

# PART FOUR

## SOURCES OF HERALDIC DESIGN

The designing of heraldry is essentially a derivative art. It does not call so much for originality in the designer as for nice judgement, balance and a sense of pattern. As the grammar of heraldry developed it became increasingly elaborate and detailed. The most refreshing sources of inspiration may be found in the study of the simpler early historical examples of those arts and crafts in which heraldry was used. Modern craftsmen will of course find interest in the development of contemporary heraldic design. But as the roots of heraldry lie in the past so do the majority of lively and satisfying examples of heraldic art. No designer can hope to develop his taste and knowledge without an interest in this early work, and it is excellent practice for the beginner to make copies of fine work.

The grammar and science of heraldry can be learned from manuals, but the designing is too complex to master merely from books and few art schools attempt to teach the subject in design courses. When modern craftsmen combine a knowledge of heraldry with technical skill their products can be admirable. It is therefore the more disappointing that the subject of heraldic design is not taken sufficiently seriously to ensure competence. The designing of arms appears to be deceptively easy, but modern examples often reveal a lack of understanding of the structure and rules of insignia, and a weak sense of design as a whole.

### PLACES

Students living in or near London are fortunate in the range of material available for study. There are splendid examples of surviving heraldic art to be seen from the Middle Ages to the present day and the British Museum, the Victoria and Albert Museum and the Public Record Office are all rich in examples of armorial designs in many different media. Westminster Abbey is alone a wonderful source book for the development and use of heraldry on monuments and the changing styles of different periods. The play of light and shade on carved heraldry enriches its beauty and gives the observer a better grasp of the subject than the study of photographs alone can do. Hampton Court is a particular field for the study of Tudor heraldry.

Within range of London there are many places of interest to the student, particularly St. George's Chapel at Windsor, which has the magnificent series of early Garter stall plates among its heraldic riches. The colleges of Oxford and Cambridge are notable sources of varied heraldic design in stone and metal and glass. Parish churches are hunting grounds for typical examples of heraldry on brasses, hatchments and sculptured monuments of all periods including the later and more decadent styles. But it is the great cathedrals all over England that are often the most rich and absorbing fields of study for the eager student, and of these Canterbury is the most outstanding in the variety of heraldic design to be seen there. The 'Stately Homes' on view to the public usually contain interesting heraldic designs on architecture and on personal possessions, but unfortunately there is rarely time for detailed study during normal tours of these houses.

## SEALS

As heraldry was originally a system of personal identification, its use was well developed for smaller objects of a personal nature, especially seals. When few people could read and write the seal had more value than a signature. In fact a great deal of the history as well as the artistic development of heraldic design can be learnt from surviving seals, especially those of the 13th and 14th centuries. From the 12th century when heraldry began to be systematized, the development of shield-shapes, the treatment of crests and the origin and use of supporters can be traced in the spirited treatment of armorial devices by early seal engravers who were themselves expert craftsmen producing designs of astonishing beauty and life. The Great Seals of the realm embody the romantic concept of the armed and crested prince with shield and sword, his surcoat and the bardings of his galloping charger moving in the wind of their speed, all richly emblazoned with heraldic devices. A small selection of seals is on view in the British Museum including some of the Great Seals and a few fine ecclesiastical seals. The British Museum holds a splendid collection of seals which are described in Birch's Catalogue. The Public Record Office also has a fine collection of seals; those attached to the Baron's Letter of 1301 should be especially noted. Local archives and museums are also a source for study.

## PERSONAL POSSESSIONS

In the houses of the wealthy armigerous families the arms of the family and kin were much used on personal possessions. Table silver, china, bookbindings, book-

Fig. 115. From an index of Armorial Bearings
c. 1446, figure representing Alderman John
Gedney, Lord Mayor of London 1427, with his
arms and those of his successors in Cornhill
Ward. Guildhall Library

plates and domestic embroideries such as bed hangings might all display the family
arms. On a larger scale carved stone armorials on gateways or on chimney breasts
were used, and arms were worked in wrought iron for fire backs and gates. Historic houses now open to the public give one a better idea of the way arms were
displayed in everyday life than seeing similar objects in museums.

## EMBROIDERY

In addition to use in domestic and personal embroideries heraldic designs have
been used for modern kneelers and hangings in many churches. St. Clement
Danes, Chelsea Old Church and Winchester and Wells, among other Cathedrals,
show examples of these.

## MANUSCRIPTS

Pictorial vellum rolls of Arms dating from 1253, and early manuscripts containing records of armorial bearings with blazons painted or tricked, may be seen at
the British Museum, the College of Arms, the Society of Antiquaries and Guildhall
Library, London. These are of value to the herald painter for the direct painting
and bold treatment of the simple early arms. (Plate 2a, Fig. 115.)

Illuminated manuscripts such as the Luttrell Psalter of c. 1340 (in the British

Museum), which depicts Sir Geoffrey Luttrell in his splendid trappings, contain exquisite pictures of shields of arms.

# MEMORIALS

## STALL PLATES

To commemorate knights of the Orders of Chivalry stall plates of engraved enamelled metal were affixed to the panelling of the stalls of the knights in the chapels of the Orders. Of these the early stall plates of some seven hundred of the Knights of the Garter in St. George's Chapel at Windsor, are superb examples of late medieval art. The banners suspended above the stalls bear the arms of the living knights of the Order and are removed at their death. In Westminster Abbey there are stall plates of the knights of the Order of the Bath; later in date, these are not nearly so outstanding in design, nor are those of St. Michael and St. George in St. Paul's Cathedral. The stall plates of the Royal Victorian Order are in the Queen's Chapel of the Savoy.

## HERALDRY ON MONUMENTS

In spite of the great loss of ecclesiastical sculpture during the iconoclastic periods of English history, there survives a number of heraldically fine tombs and monuments such as that noble bronze of Richard Beauchamp, Earl of Warwick c. 1454, in the Beauchamp chapel at Warwick; the tomb of the Black Prince at Canterbury and the Percy monument in Beverley Minster. In Westminster Abbey the memorials on many of the splendid monuments have been repainted and recently gilded.

This use of heraldry on the tombs of the great and also on memorial brasses was widespread, and forms one of the principal sources of information on the subject. It is closely allied to the development of armour and costume and the study of tombs and effigies will enhance the student's interest in these. Stained glass is another craft in which heraldic design plays an apt and brilliant role and there are fine modern examples.

# THE ROYAL BEASTS

A modern set of 'The Queen's Beasts' were made in plaster by James Woodford, R.A., for the Coronation of Queen Elizabeth II and can now be seen at Hampton Court Palace. These ten creatures, each six feet high, bear shields of arms and badges in colour. Uncoloured replicas in stone stand in Kew Gardens and with their humour and dignity add to the pictorial effect of the landscape.

Fig. 116. Sir John Harsick and his Lady, *d.* 1384. A brass at Southacre, Norfolk

A series of Royal Beasts guard the bridge over the moat at Hampton Court. They were placed there in 1910.

Royal creatures may also be seen on roof bosses in St. George's Chapel, Windsor. Those that decorate the buttresses and parapet are modern and were erected in 1925.

# HERALDRY IN MODERN LIFE

Craftsmen whose interest in heraldry has been awakened soon find that armorial devices are to be seen everywhere in the streets of cities and towns and on modern buildings, and are not only to be found in ancient churches and colleges.    Arms are displayed outside banks, the offices of insurance companies, business premises and on the shop fascias of Royal Warrant holders.    Shipping companies, railways, airways, gas, electricity and atomic energy concerns and many more corporate bodies have arms and frequently display them with éclat.    The ancient custom of using signs outside inns has been revived and many of these are appropriately heraldic in design.    County councils, city and town councils and city livery companies use heraldic seals on documents; they display their arms on public buildings and sometimes on bridges and on road signs.    Some outstanding works in silver and precious metals have been made in this century for public bodies such as these.    Universities, colleges, schools and societies bear arms and badges and use them not only on their buildings but on a smaller scale on blazers and even on ties.    The art and science of heraldry is certainly in evidence in modern life, it fills the need for display and tradition in a unique way.

# THE HERALDRY SOCIETY

Membership of the Society is open to all who are interested in the subject.    The aims of the Society are the encouragement and extension of interest in, and knowledge of, heraldry, armoury, chivalry, genealogy and kindred subjects.    The Society publishes the only national heraldic magazine in Great Britain—'The Coat of Arms'; this and other publications by the Society have much to offer the designer of heraldry.    The address of the Heraldry Society is 59 Gordon Square, London, W.C.I.

# BOOKS

There are many books about heraldry and the craftsman in search of information may well feel bewildered with such a wide choice in front of him.    Anyone seeking a broad introduction to the subject should first read the notable article on

Heraldry by Oswald Barron in the 11th and subsequent editions of the 'Encyclopaedia Britannica'. Heraldic art, grammar and law are different in Britain from the rest of Europe both in the style of drawing and the composition of arms, and also in the usages to which arms are subject. In 'Chambers' Encyclopaedia' Sir Anthony Wagner writes on 'Heraldry in Britain', D. L. Galbreath on 'Continental Heraldry' and H. Stanford London on 'Heraldic Terminology'.

The subsequent short list of books includes a selection of those on the grammar and rules that are essential to a knowledge of heraldry.

There are comparatively few books on heraldry as an art but of these 'Heraldry for Craftsmen and Designers' by W. H. St. John Hope, first published in 1913, is indispensable. The admirable illustrations include some of the best heraldic work of the Middle Ages, with the emphasis on seals, Garter stall plates and early monuments. One could wish that this truly invaluable book could be brought up to date incorporating better photographs of early heraldry and good examples of modern work.

The artist G. W. Eve, who helped to raise the standard of heraldic design at the beginning of this century, wrote two most useful books: 'Decorative Heraldry' published in 1892, and 'Heraldry as Art' in 1907. These are illustrated with many examples of applied heraldry through the centuries; unfortunately both books have been out of print for some time and although library copies may be consulted the enthusiastic designer will wish to have copies of his own.

The present writer owes a great debt to these authors, who first fired her interest in heraldry when a student and to whom she owes an obligation to which this book is itself a witness.

## LIST OF BOOKS

This brief bibliography includes only those books considered to be of help to heraldic designers.

*Decorative Heraldry.* G. W. Eve. George Bell & Sons. 1892

*Heraldry as Art.* G. W. Eve. Batsford. 1907

*Heraldry for Craftsmen and Designers.* W. H. St. John Hope. Pitman. 1913

*A Grammar of English Heraldry.* W. H. St. John Hope. Second edition revised by Anthony R. Wagner. Cambridge University Press. 1953

*Heraldry in England.* A. R. Wagner. King Penguin. 1946

*Historic Heraldry of Great Britain.* A. R. Wagner. 1948

*Complete Guide to Heraldry.*   A. C. Fox-Davies.   Nelson

*Boutell's Heraldry.*   Revised by C. W. Scott-Giles.   Warne & Co.   1963

*The Romance of Heraldry.*   C. W. Scott-Giles.   Dent.   1951

*Civic Heraldry of England and Wales.*   C. W. Scott-Giles.   1953

*Bearing of Coat Armour by Ladies.*   C. H. Francklyn.   1923

*Leopards of England.*   E. E. Dorling.   Constable.   1912

*Heraldry of the Church.*   E. E. Dorling.   Mowbray & Co.   1911

*The Stall Plates of the Knights of the Order of the Garter.*   W. H. St. John Hope.
    Constable.   1901

*Intelligible Heraldry.*   Sir Christopher Lynch-Robinson, Bt., and Adrian Lynch-
    Robinson.   Macdonald.   1947

*Scots Heraldry.*   Sir Thomas Innes of Learney.   Oliver & Boyd.   1955

*Simple Heraldry Cheerfully Illustrated.*   Iain Moncreiffe and Don Pottinger.   Nelson.
    1953

*The Colour of Heraldry.*   A publication of the Heraldry Society.   1958

*European Armour.*   Claude Blair.   Batsford.   1958

*Royal Beasts.*   H. Stanford London.   Produced by the Heraldry Society.   1956

*The Queen's Beasts.*   H. Stanford London.   Newman Neame.   1953

*The Coat of Arms* (quarterly).   Published by the Heraldry Society

*The Armorial Bearings of the Guilds of London.*   John Bromley and Heather Child.
    Warne & Co.   1960

Among works of a comprehensive character which include good photographs of
heraldic sculpture are:

*English Medieval Sculpture.*   Arthur Gardner.   Cambridge University Press.   1951

*Sculpture in Britain in the Middle Ages.*   Lawrence Stone.   Penguin History of
    Art.   1955

# INDEX